Intermediate 2

ISBN 0-7398-8798-X

Copyright © 2004 Steck-Vaughn, a division of Harcourt Supplemental Publishers, Inc.

All rights reserved. No part of the material protected by this copyright may be reproduced or utilized in any form or by any means, electronic or mechanical, including photocopying, recording, or by any information storage and retrieval system, without permission in writing from the copyright owner. Requests for permission to make copies of any part of the work should be mailed to: Copyright Permissions, Steck-Vaughn Company, P.O. Box 26015, Austin, Texas 78755.

Printed in the United States of America.

1 2 3 4 5 6 7 8 9 10 030 10 09 08 07 06 05 04

www.steck-vaughn.com

Table of Contents

PRACTICE PRETEST FOR STANFORD 10
Test Battery, Intermediate 2 Level

    Mathematics Problem Solving 4

    Mathematics Procedures 18

Number Sense and Operations

Skill Focus Lessons

    Place Value 28

    Represent Numbers: Fractions 29

    Represent Numbers: Decimals 30

    Compare and Order Numbers 31

    Round Numbers 32

    Add and Subtract Decimals 33

    Add and Subtract Fractions 34

    Multiply Fractions 35

    Order of Operations 36

    Number Sentences 37

    Estimation 38

    Problem Solving 39

Skill Review: Number Sense and Operations 40

Patterns, Relationships, and Algebra

Skill Focus Lessons

    Patterns 44

    Algebraic Expressions and Equations 45

Skill Review: Patterns, Relationships, and Algebra 46

Data, Statistics, and Probability

Skill Focus Lessons
Interpret Graphs: Charts and Pictographs 48
Interpret Graphs: Bar Graphs and Circle Graphs 49
Mean, Median, Mode, and Range 50
Combinations 51
Identify Possible Outcomes 52
Probability 53

Skill Review: Data, Statistics, and Probability 54

Geometry and Measurement

Skill Focus Lessons
The Coordinate Plane 58
Spatial Reasoning: Plane Figures 59
Spatial Reasoning: Solid Figures 60
Transformations 61
Units of Measure: Length 62
Perimeter 63
Time 64
Scale Drawings 65

Skill Review: Geometry and Measurement 66

PRACTICE POSTTEST FOR STANFORD 10
Test Battery, Intermediate 2 Level

Mathematics Problem Solving 70
Mathematics Procedures 85

Test Materials

Reference Sheet 94
Centimeter and Inch Ruler 95

Mathematics Problem Solving

DIRECTIONS

Read each question or problem carefully. Then answer the question or work the problem. Mark the space for your answer.

SAMPLE A

What is the value of the 5 in 26,853?

- A. 5
- B. 50
- C. 500
- D. 5000

SAMPLE B

Yellow   Yellow

Red   Green

What fraction of the marbles are red?

- A. $\frac{1}{4}$
- B. $\frac{1}{2}$
- C. $\frac{1}{3}$
- D. $\frac{3}{4}$

---

1 The chart below shows the scores that four members of the diving team received for their first-round dives.

Diving Scores

Name	Score
Andy	9.21
Bob	9.87
Charlie	9.36
Zeb	8.95

Who received the *highest* score?

- A. Andy
- B. Bob
- C. Charlie
- D. Zeb

2 Which digit in the decimal number 28.307 is in the thousandths place?

- A. 0
- B. 3
- C. 7
- D. 8

Mathematics Problem Solving

3

For her birthday, Maude received a book, a card, a bouquet of flowers, and a bottle of perfume. These gifts were from Phil, Diana, Angelica, and Veronica. Diana did *not* give her the card or the perfume. Angelica gave Maude the flowers. The card was from a woman. Who gave Maude perfume for her birthday?

Phil	Diana	Angelica	Veronica
A	B	C	D

4

Frida is arranging 28 stuffed animals on her shelves. She wants each shelf to have the same number of stuffed animals. On how many shelves can Frida arrange her stuffed animals?

5	6	7	8
A	B	C	D

5

A grain of salt is approximately 4 thousandths of an inch in length. Which number is equal to 4 thousandths?

4.0	0.4	0.04	0.004
A	B	C	D

6

Sharon has between $5\frac{7}{8}$ feet and 6 feet of fishing line left in her tackle box. Which number could represent the length of fishing line in her tackle box?

5.85	5.9	6.05	6.1
A	B	C	D

Pretest

Mathematics Problem Solving

7

Velma bought 12 new books at the bookstore. Of her new books, 5 are mysteries, 4 are science fiction, 2 are literature, and 1 is poetry. About what percent of Velma's new books are science fiction?

12%	20%	33%	45%
A	B	C	D

8

The walk from Juan's house to school is 1.91 miles. The walk from Jessica's house to school is 1.06 miles. Which statement *best* describes the distance Juan walks to school?

A Juan walks about half as far as Jessica.

B Juan walks about twice as far as Jessica.

C Juan walks about the same distance as Jessica.

D Juan walks almost three times as far as Jessica.

9

The drawing below shows the tile pattern on Michael's parents's new kitchen floor.

What fraction of the pattern is orange?

$\frac{1}{9}$	$\frac{2}{3}$	$\frac{1}{3}$	$\frac{4}{9}$
A	B	C	D

10

Which fraction is equivalent to $\frac{3}{5}$?

$\frac{9}{30}$	$\frac{15}{30}$	$\frac{16}{30}$	$\frac{18}{30}$
A	B	C	D

Mathematics Problem Solving

11. Coach Nelson brought a case of 24 cans of juice to the softball game. By the end of the game, there were only 6 cans of juice left. What fraction of the case of juice is left?

$\frac{1}{6}$ $\frac{1}{8}$ $\frac{1}{4}$ $\frac{1}{3}$
A   B   C   D

12. Joanna used her calculator to find the answer to $8723 \overline{)314}$. Which shows the calculator keys she pressed?

A   8723 ÷ 314 =

B   8723 × 314 =

C   314 ÷ 8723 =

D   314 = 8723 ×

13.

Julia collects stamps. She asks her aunt to guess how many stamps she has. Julia gives her aunt these clues:

The number has 3 different digits.

The tens digit is 3 more than the hundreds digit.

The tens digit is 3 times the ones digit.

Which could be the number of stamps Julia has?

584   141   362   692
A   B   C   D

14. Evaluate the expression.

10 + (11 − 3) × 5

50   70   90   110
A   B   C   D

Mathematics Problem Solving

15 Jay and Ellen's mother bought 12 small boxes of cereal for their trip. At the end of the trip, there were 3 unopened boxes. Their mother had eaten 1 box, and Jay and Ellen had eaten the rest. If Jay and Ellen ate the same number of boxes of cereal, how many boxes did each of them eat?

A 10 boxes
C 5 boxes
B 7 boxes
D 4 boxes

16 $9 + 8 = 8 + 9$

What property of addition does the number sentence above show?

A Commutative Property
B Associative Property
C Distributive Property
D Identity Property

17 Clayton wants to know how much his baby brother Dylan weighs. First, Clayton steps on the scale by himself. He weighs 102 pounds. Then, he gets on the scale while holding Dylan. Their total weight is 119 pounds.

Which equation could be used to find d, Dylan's weight?

A $119 + 102 = d$
B $102 \times d = 119$
C $d = 119 - 102$
D $d + 119 = 102$

Mathematics Problem Solving

18

Maggie has this amount of play money left when she finishes playing a board game with her friends. She owes another player an amount of money that she cannot pay using only the bills she has left.

Which could be the amount Maggie owes?

$90.00 $105.00 $35.00 $75.00
  A   B   C   D

19

Jamal and Melissa have the same amount of money in coins. Melissa has 4 dimes, a quarter and 3 nickels. Jamal has only dimes. How many dimes does Jamal have?

7   8   9   10
A   B   C   D

20

Jessica used her calculator to multiply 310 × 51. But she got the wrong answer.

How did Jessica know that 1525 was wrong?

A The correct answer should end with a 3.

B The correct answer should be less than 310.

C The correct answer should end with a 0.

D The correct answer should end with a 1.

21

Kenesha wrote the following numbers:

5, 15, 45, 135, 405, 1215

She used the same rule on each number to get the next number.

What rule did Kenesha use?

A Add 5   C Multiply by 3
B Add 10   D Multiply by 5

Pretest

Mathematics Problem Solving

22 Pete bought a case of 72 tennis balls. The tennis balls were in cans that each contained three balls.

In which equation does the ☐ stand for the number of cans in the case?

A ☐ + 3 = 72   C 3 ÷ 72 = ☐

B 72 × ☐ = 3   D 72 ÷ ☐ = 3

23 Alyssa and her mother ordered 5 dozen roses to be arranged and delivered. The chart shows the florist's prices.

Blossom Florist

Prices	
1 dozen roses	$25.00
Arranging and Delivery	$2.50 per dozen

What was the total cost of Alyssa's and her mother's order?

$108.50 $127.50 $120.50 $137.50
   A   B   C   D

24 The chart below shows the prices at Lanes Bowling Center.

Lanes Bowling Center

Activity	Price
Bowling (per game)	$2.50
Shoe Rental (per pair)	$3.00
Video Arcade (per game)	$0.50

When Ricardo and his dad went bowling, they had $27.00 to spend. Each of them rented bowling shoes and bowled 3 games.

How much money do Ricardo and his dad have left?

$6.00 $5.50 $5.00 $4.50
  A   B   C   D

25 Olga and Linus ran against each other for student council president. Olga received 156 votes and Linus received 188 votes. If there are 367 students in the school, how many students did not vote?

20   23   26   29
 A   B   C   D

Mathematics Problem Solving

26

The input-output values for Y and Z form a pattern.

Y	Z
9	5
11	7
12	8
13	9

What is the rule for the pattern?

- A. Y × 4
- B. Y − 4
- C. Y + 4
- D. Y ÷ 4

27

The United States House of Representatives has 435 members. In some cases, $\frac{2}{3}$ of the members must agree. How many members make up $\frac{2}{3}$ of the U.S. House of Representatives?

- A. 240
- B. 267
- C. 290
- D. 311

28

$g = 78 \div 13$

What is the value of g?

- A. 6
- B. 7
- C. 8
- D. 9

29

Jenna constructs and paints birdhouses as a hobby. The number of pints of paint needed for different numbers of birdhouses is shown in the table.

Number of Birdhouses	4	8	12	16	20
Pints of Paint	2	4	6	8	10

What is the *greatest* number of birdhouses Jenna can paint if she has 7 pints of paint?

- A. 6
- B. 10
- C. 14
- D. 18

Mathematics Problem Solving

30

Which expression represents the total distance from point A to point B?

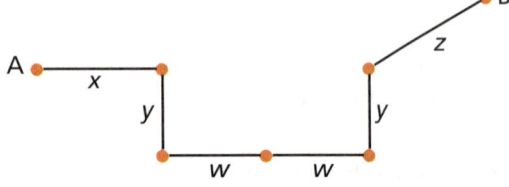

A $x + y + z + w$ **C** $2(x + y + z + w)$

B $x + 2w + y + z$ **D** $x + 2w + 2y + z$

31

This chart shows the number of dogs the Pet Adoption Group placed into new families last week.

Dogs Placed Last Week

Day	Number of Dogs
Sunday	3
Monday	2
Tuesday	5
Wednesday	4
Thursday	4
Friday	7
Saturday	10

What is the mode of the number of dogs placed by the group?

4   5   8   10
A   B   C   D

32

Fred, Sam, and their grandfather want to go to the movies. The chart below shows the prices for two of the movie theaters in town.

Movie Theater Prices

Age Category	Mall Multiplex	Discount Cinema
Child (under 12)	$4.50	$1.50
Teen (12–17)	$6.00	$2.50
Adult (18–64)	$8.25	$5.50
Senior (65+)	$4.00	$2.00

Fred is 10 years old, Sam is 13 years old, and their grandfather is 68 years old. How much money will they save if they go to Discount Cinema instead of the Mall Multiplex?

$6.00 $8.25 $8.50 $14.50
A   B   C   D

Mathematics Problem Solving

33

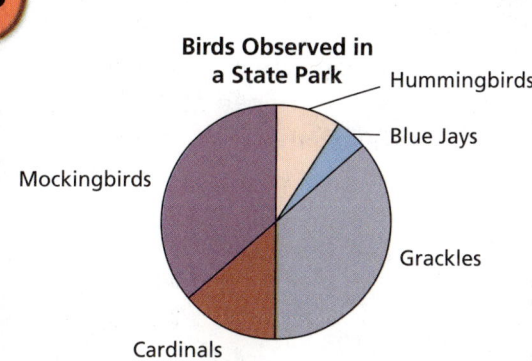

Birds Observed in a State Park

Which shows the correct data for the circle graph above?

A
Mockingbirds	50%
Grackles	50%
Cardinals	25%
Hummingbirds	25%
Blue Jays	10%

B
Mockingbirds	35%
Grackles	35%
Cardinals	15%
Hummingbirds	10%
Blue Jays	5%

C
Mockingbirds	20%
Grackles	20%
Cardinals	20%
Hummingbirds	20%
Blue Jays	20%

D
Mockingbirds	10%
Grackles	10%
Cardinals	25%
Hummingbirds	25%
Blue Jays	30%

34

The stem-and-leaf plot shows the number of students that attended each safety patrol meeting during the year.

Number of Students

1	5 6 9
2	1 3 6 6 7
3	0 4 5

Key: 1 | 5 means 15

How many meetings were attended by at *least* 23 students?

1	4	5	7
A	B	C	D

35

Greg and Caroline are working on a new bulletin board. They buy a package of pushpins that has 25 white pins, 25 blue pins, 25 red pins, 25 green pins, and 25 yellow pins. They use all the yellow pins first. Then, without looking, Greg pulls a pin out of the package and hands it to Caroline. What is the probability that it is red?

$\frac{1}{5}$	$\frac{1}{4}$	$\frac{1}{100}$	$\frac{1}{25}$
A	B	C	D

Pretest

36

Ernie traced a pattern to draw Figure P on the graph. He then moved the pattern one time to draw Figure Q.

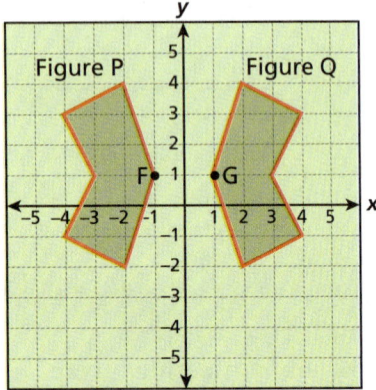

What transformation did Ernie use when he moved the pattern to draw Figure Q?

A A reflection (flip) across the *x*-axis

B A translation (slide) to the right

C A rotation (turn) around point F

D A reflection (flip) across the *y*-axis

37

Liza got a box with an interesting shape. She cut it open along its edges and got this shape.

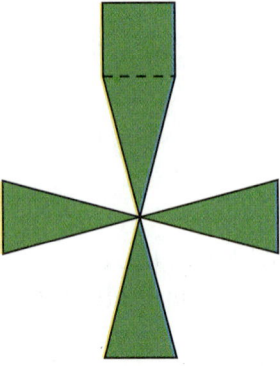

Based on the shape she got, what did the box look like before she cut it open?

A 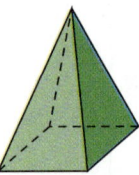   C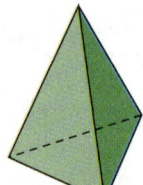

B 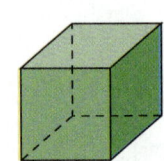   D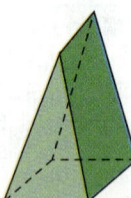

Mathematics Problem Solving

38 Mrs. Archer, the school counselor, asked all fifth-grade students to record how many hours of television they watched in one week. She used the information to make this graph.

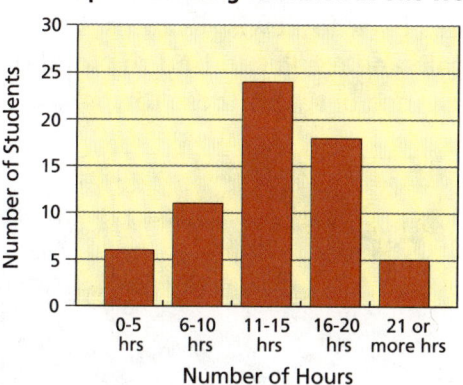

What is the total number of students who watched television at *least* 11 hours in one week?

17	24	47	64
A	B	C	D

39 Carmen's sister wears a uniform to work. Her pants are either brown, beige, or blue. Her four shirts are blue, brown, plaid, and striped. How many different combinations of one pair of pants and one shirt does Carmen's sister have?

7	12	16	24
A	B	C	D

40 Eight children are playing outside. Six of the children are not related and two are twins. One of the twins stops playing and goes home. If a child is picked at random from the remaining children, what is the probability that the chosen child is the chosen other twin?

$\frac{1}{8}$	$\frac{1}{7}$	$\frac{1}{4}$	$\frac{1}{2}$
A	B	C	D

41

Which shapes could be put together to make the figure shown above?

A

B

C

D

Pretest 15

Mathematics Problem Solving

42

Use your centimeter ruler to answer this question.

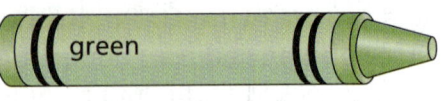

How much longer is the green crayon than the red crayon?

1 cm	1.5 cm	2 cm	3 cm
A	**B**	**C**	**D**

43

Eric has a gallon jug of water that is about $\frac{3}{4}$ full. He knows there are 16 fluid ounces in a pint and 8 pints in a gallon. About how many fluid ounces are in Eric's jug?

A 48 fluid ounces

B 64 fluid ounces

C 96 fluid ounces

D 128 fluid ounces

44

Use your standard ruler to measure to the nearest quarter inch and the map below to answer this question.

Ryan takes a bus trip to three towns to visit relatives. His trip takes him from Lewis to Dalton to Tyler. From Tyler he goes back to Lewis. Ryan uses the map scale and a ruler to find the total direct distance between these towns.

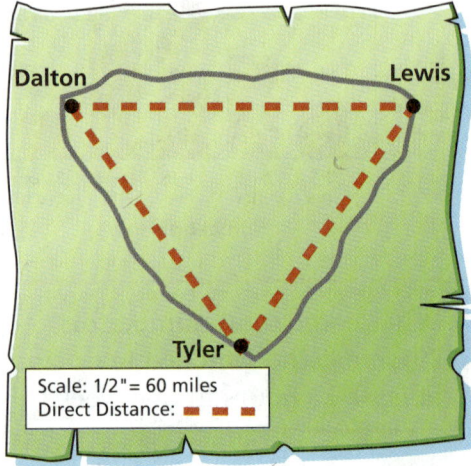

How many total miles did Ryan travel on the bus trip?

A 540 mi

B 570 mi

C 580 mi

D 600 mi

Mathematics Problem Solving

45

A map has a scale of 1 inch = 50 miles. The distance on the map from Centerville to Pleasantville is 6 inches.

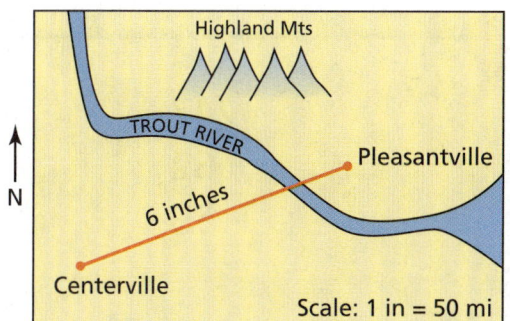

What is the actual distance from Centerville to Pleasantville?

A 350 miles
B 300 miles
C 56 miles
D 30 miles

46

Isabel went to Heather's house at 10:05 A.M. Heather's brother told Isabel that Heather left the house at 8:45 A.M. to go to her math tutor. How long had Heather been gone before Isabel arrived?

A 1 hour 30 minutes
B 55 minutes
C 1 hour 10 minutes
D 1 hour 20 minutes

47

Oscar's Paper Route

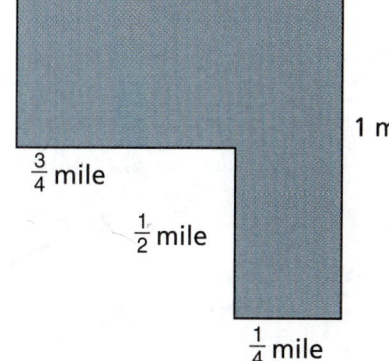

The perimeter of the figure above shows Oscar's newspaper delivery route.

How far does Oscar ride his bike each day to deliver newspapers?

A 4 miles
B $4\frac{1}{2}$ miles
C $5\frac{1}{4}$ miles
D 6 miles

48

Which unit would be best to measure the amount of soup in a bowl?

A Cups
B Milliliters
C Grams
D Gallons

Mathematics Procedures

DIRECTIONS ▶

Read each question or problem carefully. Then answer the question or work the problem. Mark the space for your answer. If a correct answer is not here, mark the space for NH.

SAMPLE A

$$42.7 + 6.6$$

- A 36.1
- B 48.3
- C 49.3
- D 50.2
- E NH

SAMPLE B

A community swimming pool is divided into two sections, one for adults and one for children. The adults' pool holds 19,250 gallons of water. The children's pool holds 4650 gallons of water.

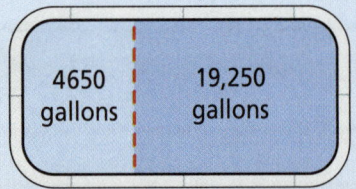

How much more water does the adults' pool hold?

- A 13,600 gallons
- B 14,400 gallons
- C 15,400 gallons
- D 15,600 gallons
- E NH

1

$$247 \\ 62 \\ + 59$$

- A 321
- B 358
- C 361
- D 368
- E NH

2

$$23 \times 45$$

- A 935
- B 1035
- C 965
- D 945
- E NH

Mathematics Procedures

3

0.75 × 8 = ☐

- A 0.06
- B 0.6
- C 6
- D 60
- E NH

5

42.09 − 14.92 = ☐

- A 27.17
- B 27.07
- C 26.17
- D 26.07
- E NH

4

604 ÷ 7 = ☐

- A 83 R3
- B 86 R2
- C 89 R1
- D 86
- E NH

6

2474 − 536 = ☐

- A 2142
- B 1948
- C 3010
- D 2038
- E NH

Pretest

Mathematics Procedures

7. $\frac{3}{8} \times 24 = \square$

A $\frac{1}{64}$
B $\frac{1}{9}$
C 6
D 9
E 64

9. $29.08 - 13.23 = \square$

A 15.85
B 15.75
C 16.25
D 16.75
E NH

8. $2.11 \times 7.3 = \square$

A 12.803
B 10.303
C 14.703
D 15.403
E NH

10. $67.5 \div 5 = \square$

A 13.5
B 11.1
C 12.9
D 13.8
E NH

Mathematics Procedures

11

$$\frac{5}{9} - \frac{3}{9} = \square$$

A $\frac{1}{9}$

B $\frac{2}{9}$

C $\frac{8}{18}$

D $\frac{2}{18}$

E 2

13

$$2\frac{4}{5} + 3\frac{3}{5} = \square$$

A $5\frac{5}{7}$

B $6\frac{5}{7}$

C $6\frac{2}{5}$

D $5\frac{7}{10}$

E $5\frac{1}{5}$

12

$$28 \times \frac{1}{7} = \square$$

A 196

B $28\frac{1}{7}$

C $4\frac{1}{7}$

D $7\frac{1}{28}$

E 4

14

$$\frac{4}{9} \times \frac{3}{2} = \square$$

A $\frac{1}{7}$

B $\frac{8}{27}$

C $\frac{27}{8}$

D $\frac{2}{3}$

E $\frac{7}{18}$

Pretest

Mathematics Procedures

15

$$\frac{5}{9} - \frac{2}{6} = \square$$

A $\frac{3}{3}$

B $\frac{3}{6}$

C $\frac{2}{9}$

D $\frac{3}{9}$

E $\frac{5}{18}$

16

$$2.45 \div 7 = \square$$

A 35

B 3.5

C 0.35

D 0.035

E NH

17

Erin gathers 198 apples from the trees in her yard. She keeps $\frac{4}{9}$ of the apples and gives the rest to the local food bank.

How many apples does Erin keep?

A 86

B 88

C 110

D 118

E NH

Mathematics Procedures

18

Corey earns $0.13 for every newspaper he delivers. Today he delivers 140 newspapers.

How much money does Corey earn today?

A $13.20
B $14.20
C $18.20
D $27.20
E NH

19

Rita wants to drive her truck across this bridge. Her truck weighs 28,500 pounds.

WEIGHT LIMIT 54,000 POUNDS

What is the most weight Rita can carry in her truck and still be able to drive across the bridge?

A 2550 pounds
B 15,500 pounds
C 25,000 pounds
D 25,500 pounds
E NH

20

Andrew is 1 of 9 workers at a small company. Each month, the workers receive an equal share of the company's profits. If the company makes a profit of $23,130 this month, how much of the profit will Andrew receive?

A $2810   D $2790
B $2570   E NH
C $2750

Pretest   23

Mathematics Procedures

21 Tony and Angelo eat lunch together. Tony's meal costs $6.45. Angelo's meal costs $1.65 less than the cost of Tony's meal.

What is the cost of Angelo's meal?

A $4.80
B $4.90
C $5.90
D $8.10
E NH

22 A bag of salted peanuts contains 480 mg of salt. The recommended daily allowance of salt for healthy adults is 2400 mg. What fraction of the daily allowance of salt is contained in the bag of peanuts?

A $\frac{1}{5}$ D $\frac{1}{2}$

B $\frac{1}{4}$ E $\frac{0}{1}$

C $\frac{1}{3}$

23 Leo goes to school from 8:20 A.M. to 3:15 P.M. every day.

How much time does Leo spend at school every day?

A 6 hours 45 minutes
B 6 hours 55 minutes
C 7 hours 5 minutes
D 7 hours 55 minutes
E NH

Mathematics Procedures

24

Mrs. Porter pays $68.75 for 25 tickets to the zoo. Each ticket costs the same amount.

What is the cost of each ticket?

A $1.95
B $2.75
C $3.75
D $6.85
E NH

25

Ron and Jean each eat $\frac{2}{5}$ of a submarine sandwich. What fractional part of the sandwich was left?

A $\frac{4}{5}$
B $\frac{3}{5}$
C $\frac{2}{5}$
D $\frac{1}{5}$
E $\frac{0}{5}$

26

Leslie delivers 28 stacks of newspapers to a store. There are 15 newspapers in each stack.

How many newspapers does Leslie deliver?

A 42
B 43
C 285
D 340
E NH

Mathematics Procedures

27

A small bag of dried fruit weighs 1.74 ounces. A box contains 24 bags of dried fruit.

What is the weight in ounces of the 24 bags of dried fruit?

A 12.83 ounces
B 24.98 ounces
C 41.76 ounces
D 43.96 ounces
E NH

28

A nickel has a mass of 5 grams and a penny has a mass of 2.27 grams.

5 grams   2.27 grams

How much more mass does the nickel have than the penny?

A 2.83 grams
B 2.73 grams
C 3.62 grams
D 3.63 grams
E NH

29

Julie surveyed 189 students at her school. She found that $\frac{5}{7}$ of the students surveyed buy lunch at school. How many of the students that Julie surveyed buy lunch at school?

A 89
B 135
C 152
D 124
E NH

Mathematics Procedures

30

Tom recorded the colors of the cars in the parking lot at school. He found that $\frac{1}{8}$ were white and $\frac{1}{4}$ were black.

What fractional part of the cars in the lot are either white or black?

A $\frac{3}{8}$

B $\frac{2}{12}$

C $\frac{2}{8}$

D $\frac{1}{12}$

E $\frac{2}{4}$

31

On Friday 43 people visited a museum, 97 visited on Saturday, and 185 visited on Sunday. What is the total number of people who visited the museum on Friday, Saturday, and Sunday?

A 215

B 225

C 305

D 315

E NH

32

Dan drank $3\frac{5}{8}$ cups of water in the morning and $2\frac{7}{8}$ cups of water in the afternoon.

How many cups of water did Dan drink?

A $5\frac{1}{2}$

B $5\frac{5}{8}$

C $6\frac{1}{4}$

D $6\frac{1}{2}$

E $6\frac{7}{8}$

Pretest

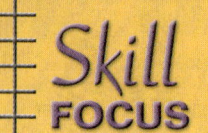

Number Sense and Operations

Place Value

The value of each digit in a number depends on its place, or position, in the number. Each place has a value that is a power of 10. Look at the number 2,472,195. Set up a place-value chart to help you find the value of each digit in the number.

millions	hundred thousands	ten thousands	thousands	hundreds	tens	ones
1,000,000	100,000	10,000	1000	100	10	1
2	4	7	2	1	9	5

Use the place-value chart to write this number in *expanded form*.
2,000,000 + 400,000 + 70,000 + 2000 + 100 + 90 + 1
Use this information to find the value of the digits. For example, the value of the digit 7 in the number 2,472,195 is 7 ten thousands, or 7 × 10,000, or 70,000.

A place-value chart can help you understand decimal numbers.

tens	ones	and	tenths	hundredths	thousandths
0	9	.	3	8	1

Use the place-value chart to write 9.381 in expanded form.
9 + 0.3 + 0.08 + 0.001
Use this information to find the value of the digits. For example, the value of the digit 8 is 8 hundredths, or 8 × 0.01, or 0.08.

> **Remember**
> When you place a 0 to the left of the decimal point as a place holder, it does not change the value of the decimal.
> Example:
> .45 = 0.45

Example

Use this number to fill in the blanks below.

70,519.264

_____ is in the tens place. Its value is _____.
_____ is in the hundreds place. Its value is _____.
_____ is in the hundredths place. Its value is _____.

Answer: 1, 10; 5, 500; 6, 0.06

ten thousands	thousands	hundreds	tens	ones	and	tenths	hundredths	thousandths
7	0	5	1	9	.	2	6	4

Number Sense and Operations

Represent Numbers: Fractions

A fraction is a number that names a part of a whole. The numerator names the number of equal parts being considered. The denominator names the total number of equal parts. The circle shown has 3 shaded parts out of 8 equal parts.

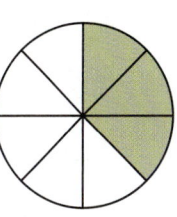

$\frac{3}{8}$ numerator / denominator

If the numerator and the denominator of a fraction have 1 as their greatest common factor (GCF), the fraction is in simplest form.

Look at the fraction $\frac{3}{8}$. The GCF is 1, so $\frac{3}{8}$ is in simplest form.

Use these steps to simplify fractions.

Proper Fraction	Improper Fraction	Mixed Number
$\frac{12}{15} = \frac{12 \div 3}{15 \div 3} = \frac{4}{5}$	$\frac{9}{3} = 9 \div 3 = 3$	$\frac{11}{5} = 11 \div 5 = 2 \text{ R}1$
Factors of 12: 1, 2, 3,…	Divide the numerator by the denominator.	Divide the numerator by the denominator.
Factors of 15: 1, 3, 5,…		Express the R1 as $\frac{1}{5}$
The GCF is 3.		$\frac{11}{5} = 2\frac{1}{5}$

To express a fraction as a decimal, divide the numerator of the fraction by its denominator.

Example: $\frac{2}{5} = 2 \div 5 = 0.4$

Remember

A *proper fraction* has a numerator that is less than its denominator.
Example: $\frac{3}{7}$

An *improper fraction* has a numerator that is greater than or equal to its denominator.
Example: $\frac{6}{5}$

A *mixed number* contains a whole number and a fraction.
Example: $4\frac{5}{8}$

Example

What fraction of the numbers on the spinner are even numbers? Express the answer as a fraction and a decimal.

There are 10 numbers. Five numbers are even: 2, 4, 6, 8 and 10. So $\frac{5}{10}$ of the spinner has even numbers.

$\frac{5}{10} = 5 \div 10 = 0.5$

Answer: $\frac{5}{10}$, 0.5

Number Sense and Operations

Represent Numbers: Decimals

Decimals are special fractions with denominators that are powers of ten.

The model represents the number $\frac{3}{10}$. To represent $\frac{3}{10}$ as a decimal, write a 3 in the tenths place: 0.3. Read the number as "three tenths".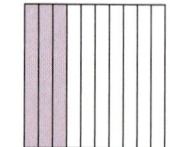

The model represents the number $1\frac{46}{100}$. To represent $1\frac{46}{100}$ as a decimal, write a 1 in the ones place, a 4 in the tenths place, and a 6 in the hundreths place: 1.46. Read the number as "one *and* forty-six hundredths." In a decimal number, the word "and" separates the whole number from the decimal.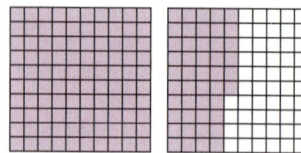

Remember
Standard form expresses a number using digits.
Example: 75.23
Word form expresses a number in words.
Example: seventy-five and twenty-three hundredths

Example

What number does the model represent?
Standard form: _____
Written form: _____

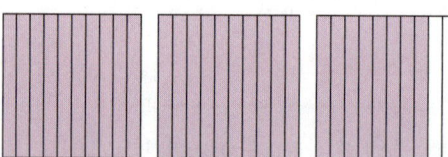

The first 2 squares are completely shaded; the whole number is 2. The third square has 8 of 10 sections shaded; the fraction is $\frac{8}{10}$.

As a decimal, the number is: 2.0 + 0.8 = 2.8. Write the word "and" between the whole number part and the decimal part: two and eight tenths.

Answer: 2.8, two and eight tenths

Number Sense and Operations

Compare and Order Numbers

Decimal Numbers To compare decimal numbers, always line up the decimal points. Compare the numbers 3.091 and 3.045.

Line up the decimal points.
   3.091
   3.045

Compare the numbers from left to right.
   $3 = 3$ $0 = 0$ $9 > 4$

The numbers are equal in the ones and tenths place. They are not equal in the hundredths place. Since $9 > 4$, $3.091 > 3.045$.

Fractions To compare fractions, the fractions must have the same denominator. Compare the fractions $\frac{1}{3}$ and $\frac{2}{9}$.

- Find the least common denominator (LCD) of $\frac{1}{3}$ and $\frac{2}{9}$. The LCD is 9.
- Express $\frac{1}{3}$ with a denominator of 9: $\frac{1}{3} = \frac{1 \times 3}{3 \times 3} = \frac{3}{9}$.
- Compare the numerators of the fractions. $3 > 2$.
- Compare the fractions. $\frac{3}{9} > \frac{2}{9}$ therefore $\frac{1}{3} > \frac{2}{9}$.

Remember
The least common denominator (LCD) of two fractions is the least common multiple (LCM) of the two denominators.
Multiples of 6: 6, <u>12</u>, 18, . . .
Multiples of 4: 4, 8, <u>12</u>, 16, . . .
The LCD of $\frac{5}{6}$ and $\frac{3}{4}$ is 12.

Example

Use the symbols $<$, $>$, or $=$ to compare these numbers.

5.2043 ___ 5.2039 $\frac{5}{8}$ ___ $\frac{2}{3}$ $\frac{4}{5}$ ___ 0.83

Compare the decimal numbers from left to right. $5 = 5$, $2 = 2$, $0 = 0$, $4 > 3$. Since $4 > 3$, $5.2043 > 5.2039$.

To compare the fractions, find the LCD of $\frac{5}{8}$ and $\frac{2}{3}$. The LCD is 24.

$\frac{5}{8} = \frac{5 \times 3}{8 \times 3} = \frac{15}{24}$. $\frac{2}{3} = \frac{2 \times 8}{3 \times 8} = \frac{16}{24}$. $\frac{15}{24} < \frac{16}{24}$, so $\frac{5}{8} < \frac{2}{3}$.

To compare the fraction and the decimal, express $\frac{4}{5}$ as a decimal.
$\frac{4}{5} = 4 \div 5 = 0.80$. $0.80 < 0.83$.

Answers: $>$, $<$, $<$

Number Sense and Operations

Round Numbers

Sometimes you do not need to use exact numbers. For example, if you want to estimate an answer, you can round the numbers in a problem. To round whole numbers or decimal numbers, follow these steps.
1. Decide what place value you will round to.
2. Look at the digit to the right of that place value.
3. If the digit is 5 or greater, round up to the higher place value. Drop all digits to the right of the rounded digit.
   If the digit is less than 5, do not change the digit in the place value. Drop all digits to the right of the rounded digit.

> **Remember**
> Adding zeros to the right of decimal digits does not change the value of a number.
> 2.68 has the same value as 2.680.

Use the steps to round these two numbers.

Round 94.68 to the nearest tenth.	Round 5735.2 to the nearest hundred.
Find the tenths place: 94.6̲8.	Find the hundreds place: 57̲35.2
Look at the digit to the right, 8.	Look at the digit to the right, 3.
Since 8 > 5, round 6 to 7 and drop the digits after 7.	Since 3 < 5, the 7 does not change, but drop the digits after the 7.
94.68 rounds to 94.7.	5735.2 rounds to 5700.

Example

Round 148.065 to the nearest hundred.
_____

Round 148.065 to the nearest hundredth.
_____

Nearest *hundred*: Find the digit in the hundreds place, 1. Look at the number to the right of 1, 4. Since 4 < 5, do not change the 1. Drop the digits to the right of 1. 148.065 rounds down to 100.

Nearest *hundredth*: Find the digit in the hundredths place, 6. Look at the number to the right of 6, 5. Since 5 = 5, round the 6 to 7. Drop the digits to the right of 7. 148.065 rounds to 148.07.

Answers: 100, 148.07

Number Sense and Operations

Add and Subtract Decimals

When adding or subtracting decimals, line up the decimal points. You may need to add zeros so that all the numbers will have the same number of decimal places. Look at these examples.

```
  16.20           25.00
   9.00         − 12.35
 + 8.04
```

When you have set up the problem, add or subtract as you would for whole numbers.

Some subtraction problems require regrouping one or more times. Remember that the rules for regrouping do not change, no matter how many times you need to regroup.

You cannot subtract 5 or 3 from 0. Starting with the ones, regroup 5 ones as 4 ones and 10 tenths. Then regroup 10 tenths as 9 tenths and 10 hundredths. Now you can subtract.

```
   4 9̄10̄10̄
   2̄5̄.0̄0̄
 − 12.35
   12.65
```

Example

Add: 23.468 + 16.82 = _____

Subtract: 37.57 − 7.86 = _____

```
   1 1
  23.468     Add from right to left: 8 + 0 = 8, 6 + 2 = 8,
+ 16.820     and 4 + 8 = 12. Regroup 12 tenths as 2 tenths and
  40.288     1 one.
             Add: 1 + 3 + 6 = 10. Regroup 10 ones as 0 ones and
             1 ten.
             Add: 1 + 2 + 1 = 4.

     16
   2 6̄ 15
  3̄7̄.5̄7̄     Subtract from right to left: 7 − 6 = 1. Regroup 7 ones
 − 7.86     as 6 ones and 10 tenths. Subtract: 15 − 8 = 7.
  29.71     Regroup 3 tens as 2 tens and 10 ones. Subtract:
            16 − 7 = 9 and 2 − 0 = 2.
```

Answers: 40.288, 29.71

Number Sense and Operations

Add and Subtract Fractions

To add or subtract fractions with the *same* denominator, simply add or subtract their numerators. Place the sum or difference over the common denominator. Simplify the answer if necessary.

$$\frac{1}{7} + \frac{3}{7} = \frac{1+3}{7} = \frac{4}{7} \qquad \frac{9}{10} - \frac{5}{10} = \frac{9-5}{10} = \frac{4}{10} = \frac{2}{5}$$

To add or subtract fractions with *different* denominators, express the fractions as equivalent fractions with a common denominator.

$$\frac{1}{6} + \frac{3}{4}$$

- Find the least common multiple (LCM) of the two denominators.
  Multiples of 6: 6, <u>12</u>, 18, 24 . . .
  Multiples of 4: 4, 8, <u>12</u>, 16, . . .

  The LCM of 6 and 4 is 12.

- Find equivalent fractions with a denominator of 12.

  $$\frac{1}{6} = \frac{1 \times 2}{6 \times 2} = \frac{2}{12} \qquad \frac{3}{4} = \frac{3 \times 3}{4 \times 3} = \frac{9}{12}$$

- Add the fractions:

  $$\frac{2}{12} + \frac{9}{12} = \frac{11}{12}.$$

Remember
Fractions are *equivalent* if they have the same value. To make an equivalent fraction, multiply the numerator and denominator by the same nonzero number.
$$\frac{1}{3} \times \frac{2}{2} = \frac{2}{6}$$
$\frac{1}{3}$ and $\frac{2}{6}$ are equivalent fractions.

Example

What is $5\frac{1}{3} - 2\frac{1}{4}$?

_____

Find a common denominator by finding the LCM of 3 and 4.

Multiples of 3: 3, 6, 9, 12, … Multiples of 4: 4, 8, 12, …
The LCM of 3 and 4 is 12. Find equivalent fractions.

$$\frac{1}{3} = \frac{1 \times 4}{3 \times 4} = \frac{4}{12} \qquad \frac{1}{4} = \frac{1 \times 3}{4 \times 3} = \frac{3}{12}$$

$$5\frac{1}{3} - 2\frac{3}{4} = 5\frac{4}{12} - 2\frac{3}{12} = 3\frac{1}{12}$$

Answer: $3\frac{1}{12}$

SKILL FOCUS

Number Sense and Operations

Multiply Fractions

You can use a model to show multiplying a fraction by a fraction.

One-half of the rectangle is shaded. One-fourth of the shaded part has lines on it. Only 1 out of 8 parts has lines on it. $\frac{1}{4}$ of $\frac{1}{2}$ is $\frac{1}{8}$.

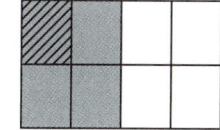

To multiply fractions, first multiply the numerators and then multiply the denominators. $\frac{2}{5} \times \frac{4}{3} = \frac{2 \times 4}{5 \times 3} = \frac{8}{15}$

To multiply a fraction by a whole number, express the whole number as a fraction with a denominator of 1. Then multiply the fractions.

$16 \times \frac{1}{4} = \frac{16}{1} \times \frac{1}{4} = \frac{16}{4} = 4$

Remember

In fraction problems, the word "of" means multiplication. For example, $\frac{1}{2}$ of 36 means $\frac{1}{2} \times 36$, or $\frac{1}{2} \times \frac{36}{1}$.

Example

Kwame painted a picture that is $\frac{2}{3}$ sky. He covered $\frac{1}{4}$ of the sky with stars. What part of his picture is sky with stars?

_____

Find $\frac{1}{4}$ of $\frac{2}{3}$. Multiply: $\frac{1}{4} \times \frac{2}{3} = \frac{2}{12} = \frac{1}{6}$.

Darla needs 12 servings of punch. If each serving is $\frac{3}{4}$ of a cup, how many cups of punch does she need?

_____

Darla needs to serve $\frac{3}{4}$ of a cup 12 times, or $\frac{3}{4} \times 12$. Express the whole number 12 as a fraction with a denominator of 1. Then multiply.

$\frac{3}{4} \times 12 = \frac{3}{4} \times \frac{12}{1} = \frac{36}{4} = 9$

Answers: $\frac{1}{6}$; 9

Number Sense and Operations

Order of Operations

To solve some number sentences you need to use more than one operation. The rules for order of operations tell the correct order in which to perform the operations.
1. Do any operations in parentheses first.
2. Multiply or divide from left to right.
3. Add or subtract from left to right.

Use the rules to find the value of this number sentence.

$$7 + 4 \times (5 - 3) - 6 = \Box$$

1. Do any operations in parentheses first.
 $7 + 4 \times (5 - 3) - 6 = 7 + 4 \times (2) - 6$
2. Multiply or divide from left to right. In some problems you will multiply first. In others you will divide first.
 $7 + 4 \times 2 - 6 = 7 + 8 - 6$
3. Add or subtract from left to right. In some problems you will add first. In others you will subtract first.
 $7 + 8 - 6 = 15 - 6 = 9$

Always add and subtract in order from left to right.

> **HINT**
>
> If you do the operations in a different order, you will get an incorrect answer. One way to remember the correct order of operations is by remembering **PMA:**
>
> **P** Parentheses
>
> **M** Multiply or divide
>
> **A** Add or subtract

Example

Use the rules for order of operations to find each answer.

$18 - 5 + 6 \times 4 = \Box$

$32 - (3 + 5) \div 2 \times 3 = \Box$

Multiply or divide:
$18 - 5 + \mathbf{6 \times 4}$

Add or subtract: $\mathbf{18 - 5} + 24$

Add or subtract: $13 + 24$

Add: $13 + 24 = 37$

Do operations in parentheses:
$32 - \mathbf{(3 + 5)} \div 2 \times 3$

Multiply or divide: $32 - \mathbf{8 \div 2} \times 3$

Multiply or divide: $32 - \mathbf{4 \times 3}$

Add or subtract: $32 - 12 = 20$

Answers: 37, 20

Number Sense and Operations

Number Sentences

One way to solve word problems is to put the words and phrases in the problem into a number sentence. Then find the answer to the problem by completing the number sentence. The chart below shows some common words and the operations they often mean.

Remember
You can use a letter to represent an unknown number in a number sentence.
Examples:
$18 + a = 26$
$(8 \times 3) - 4 \div 2 = N$

Addition (+)	plus	sum	in all	total
Subtraction (−)	minus	difference	less than	decrease
Multiplication (×)	times	product	of	per
Division (÷)	divided by	quotient	shared	equal parts

The word *twice* means multiply by 2, while *half* means divide by 2.
Word phrase: *two more than twice three is eight*.
Number sentence: $2 + 2(3) = 8$.

Tara bought 3 T-shirts for $12 each and 1 pair of sweat pants for $16. This number sentence expresses the total cost.

$$(3 \times \$12) + \$16 = \Box$$

Example

> One weekend the Nelsons planted 30 tulip bulbs. The next weekend they planted twice as many. How many bulbs, *B*, did they plant altogether?
> Write a number sentence to represent this problem.
> _____

Use the information given to write the number sentence.
One weekend the Nelsons planted 30 bulbs.
The next weekend they planted twice as many. (30×2)
The word *altogether* means you need to add. $30 + (30 \times 2)$
$30 + (30 \times 2) = B$, the number of bulbs they planted altogether.

Answer: $30 + (30 \times 2) = B$

Number Sense and Operations

Estimation

An *estimate* is a number that is close to an exact number. Some problems ask you to estimate the answer. One way to estimate an answer is to round the numbers in the problem.

Carlo lives in a small town. He takes the train into the city 18 times each month. Each round trip is 22 miles. What is a reasonable estimate for the number of miles Carlo rides the train each month?
Round 18 to 20 and 22 to 20.
Multiply the rounded numbers: 20 × 20 = 400.
Carlo rides the train *about* 400 miles each month.

Sometimes you need to decide if you need an exact or an estimated number to solve a problem. For this problem an estimated number is all you need.

Paula has $20.00 to spend at the mall. She needs to buy a $12.00 shirt. She would like to buy 3 pairs of socks. The socks cost $3.95 a pair. Can Paula buy the shirt and 3 pairs of socks?
Estimate the cost of the socks. $3.95 is almost $4.00.
Do mental math: $4.00 × 3 = $12.00, and $12.00 + $12.00 = $24.
No, Paula cannot buy the shirt and 3 pairs of socks.

HINT
Suppose your estimated answer was 43 pounds instead of 30 pounds. Since you do not know if the exact answer is less than or greater than 45 pounds, 43 might be too close to rely on an estimate. This is important because the shelf can hold only 45 pounds. In such cases, it is best to find an exact answer.

Example

A large potted plant weighs $14\frac{3}{4}$ pounds. A medium-sized one weighs $5\frac{1}{3}$ pounds. Five smaller ones weigh a little over 2 pounds each. Rita's plant shelf can hold 45 pounds. Is the shelf strong enough for these potted plants? _____

Round the weight of the plants to the nearest pound.
$14\frac{3}{4}$ rounds to 15, $5\frac{1}{3}$ rounds to 5, and 2 pounds × 5 = 10 pounds.
Add: 15 + 5 + 10 = 30.

The potted plants weigh about 30 pounds and the shelf can hold 45 pounds.

Answer: Yes, the shelf is strong enough to hold these plants.

Number Sense and Operations

Problem Solving

> **HINT**
>
> It is a good idea to estimate the answer to a word problem before finding an exact answer. This can help you decide if the answer is reasonable.

You can use a four-step problem-solving plan to solve many problems.
1. Understand the problem.
2. Make a plan to solve the problem.
3. Carry out the plan.
4. Ask yourself if the solution is reasonable.

Casey has 3 more magazines than her brother Riley. If Casey has 8 magazines, how many magazines do they have altogether?

1. Casey has 8 magazines. This is 3 more than Riley has. The problem asks how many magazines they have altogether.

2. One way to solve the problem is to write a number sentence to represent the situation.

3. Casey has 8 magazines. Riley has 8 − 3 = 5 magazines. The phrase "altogether" means addition.
   8 magazines + (8 − 3 magazines) = total number of magazines.
   8 + (8 − 3) = 8 + 5 = 13

4. If Casey and Riley had the same number of magazines they would have 8 + 8 = 16 magazines. But you know that Riley has 3 less magazines. 16 − 3 = 13, so the answer is reasonable.

Example

> Abby made 12 cups of applesauce and Jack made 15 cups of pear sauce. They mixed the two sauces together and poured them into 3 bowls. If each bowl has the same amount of sauce in it, how much sauce is in each bowl?
>
> _____
>
> One third of the sauce will go in each bowl. Write a number sentence to represent the situation.
>
> $\frac{1}{3}$ of (12 cups + 15 cups) = $\frac{1}{3} \times 27 = \frac{1}{3} \times \frac{27}{1} = \frac{27}{3}$ = 9 cups
>
> Since 3 × 9 = 27, the answer is reasonable.
>
> **Answer:** 9 cups

Number Sense and Operations

Skill Review

Number Sense and Operations

1

Which figure is $\frac{1}{4}$ shaded?

A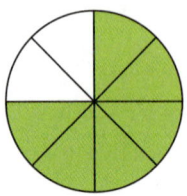

B

C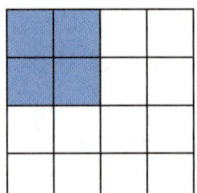

D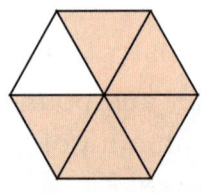

2

8024.976

Which digit is in the hundreds place?

A 8
B 7
C 6
D 0

3

Which is 190.13 in expanded form?

A 100 + 90 + 1 + 0.1 + 0.03
B 100 + 90 + 1 + 0.03
C 100 + 90 + 0.1 + 0.03
D 100 + 90 + 1 + 0.3

SKILL REVIEW

Number Sense and Operations

4

What is 2004.06 in written form?

- **A** Two thousand four and six hundredths.
- **B** Two thousand forty and six hundredths.
- **C** Two thousand four hundred and six tenths.
- **D** Two thousand four and six tenths.

5

Express 5.048 as a fraction in simplest form.

$5\frac{12}{25}$ $5\frac{12}{125}$ $5\frac{24}{25}$ $5\frac{6}{125}$

A **B** **C** **D**

6

Which fraction has a value between 1.5 and 1.75?

$1\frac{5}{8}$ $1\frac{1}{3}$ $1\frac{3}{10}$ $1\frac{2}{5}$

A **B** **C** **D**

7

What is 830.964 rounded to the nearest tenth?

- **A** 831.9
- **B** 831.0
- **C** 830.9
- **D** 830.0

8

$19.2 + 8.03 + 114.64 = \square$

- **A** 141.87
- **B** 142.14
- **C** 126.42
- **D** 119.65

9

$74\frac{1}{3} - 27\frac{1}{4} = \square$

$101\frac{7}{12}$ $47\frac{2}{7}$ $47\frac{1}{12}$ $46\frac{1}{12}$

A **B** **C** **D**

Number Sense and Operations

10. Charlie mixes $3\frac{3}{5}$ cups of water with $\frac{4}{15}$ cup of vinegar to make a cleaning solution. How many cups of cleaning solution does he have?

- A $3\frac{7}{15}$
- B $3\frac{7}{20}$
- C $3\frac{13}{15}$
- D $4\frac{2}{5}$

11. Ahmad has $2\frac{1}{2}$ cups of animal feed and 5 animals. If each animal gets the same amount of feed, how many cups of feed will each animal get?

- A $\frac{1}{2}$ cup
- B $\frac{1}{5}$ cup
- C $2\frac{1}{10}$ cups
- D 5 cups

12. Kendra ordered a pizza and ate $\frac{1}{4}$ of it. Later, her two brothers each ate half of the remaining pizza. What fraction of the total pizza did each brother eat?

- A $\frac{1}{8}$
- B $\frac{1}{4}$
- C $\frac{1}{3}$
- D $\frac{3}{8}$

13. Yesterday, Julian had $26.92. He spent $13.84 on a gift and $2.59 on wrapping paper. Which number sentence shows the amount of money, J, Julian has left?

- A $J = \$26.92 + \$13.84 + \$2.59$
- B $J = \$26.92 - \$13.84 + \$2.59$
- C $J = \$26.92 - (\$13.84 + \$2.59)$
- D $J = \$26.92 - (\$13.84 - \$2.59)$

Number Sense and Operations

14

Use the rules for order of operations to solve the problem.

$$45 \div 3 \times 5 + (7 - 2) = \square$$

- **A** 84
- **B** 80
- **C** 8
- **D** 1.5

15

Which is the *best* estimate of the product of 33.86 and 8.9?

- **A** 30
- **B** 40
- **C** 300
- **D** 350

16

Brad shared all of his candy with two friends. Brad and his two friends each got 6 pieces of candy. How many pieces of candy did Brad originally have?

- **A** 2
- **B** 6
- **C** 12
- **D** 18

Patterns, Relationships, and Algebra

Patterns

Recognizing patterns can be helpful in making predictions and solving problems. Look at the pattern below. The number of line segments in each figure is: 4, 7, 10, 13. Each new figure has 3 more line segments than the previous figure does. The rule is "add 3." The fifth figure will have 13 + 3, or 16, line segments.

Not all patterns use the addition rule. The rule for a pattern may be to subtract, multiply, or divide. Some rules combine two or more operations.

Not all patterns involve whole numbers. You might see patterns that include fractions or decimals. To find what number is next in a series of numbers, look for a pattern. Then find a rule to describe the pattern. Check to make sure the rule is followed for each step in the pattern. Use the rule to continue the pattern.

> **Remember**
> An ellipsis (. . .), or set of three dots, means that a pattern continues beyond the last number shown.
> Example:
> 1, 6, 11, 16, . . .

Example

What are the next **two** numbers in the pattern? _____

$$3\tfrac{1}{4},\ 2\tfrac{3}{4},\ 2\tfrac{1}{4},\ 1\tfrac{3}{4},\ \ldots$$

Look at the mixed numbers. The pattern shows that the numbers are decreasing in value by $\tfrac{2}{4}$. Check to see if the rule is correct:

$$3\tfrac{1}{4} - \tfrac{2}{4} = 2\tfrac{3}{4};\ 2\tfrac{3}{4} - \tfrac{2}{4} = 2\tfrac{1}{4};\ 2\tfrac{1}{4} - \tfrac{2}{4} = 1\tfrac{3}{4}.$$

Then subtract: $1\tfrac{3}{4} - \tfrac{2}{4} = 1\tfrac{1}{4}$ and $1\tfrac{1}{4} - \tfrac{2}{4} = \tfrac{3}{4}$.

Answer: $1\tfrac{1}{4}, \tfrac{3}{4}$

Patterns, Relationships, and Algebra

Algebraic Expressions and Equations

Algebra uses numbers and variables to find patterns or solve problems. A *variable* is a symbol that represents an unknown value. The symbol used is usually a letter, such as x or y.

An *algebraic expression* is a group of numbers, variables, and operation signs. An expression does *not* contain an equal sign. An example of an algebraic equation is $25 + 3x$.

An *algebraic equation* is a math sentence that always has an equal (=) sign. Equations tell you that one expression is equal to another expression. Here are two examples of algebraic equations:

$$a^2 = 35 \div 4b \qquad 28 + 3x = 2y$$

You can translate a word problem into an algebraic expression. For example: A notepad costs $2.99. Let n represent any number of notepads. The cost of n notepads is $n \times \$2.99$.

You can set up an algebraic equation to describe a word problem. For example: Box A weighs 2 pounds. The total weight of Box A and Box B is 6 pounds. Let w represent the weight of Box B. Express the weight of the two boxes using an algebraic equation.

Weight of Box A + Weight of Box B = Total weight of both boxes

If you substitute the values you know and w, you have the equation $2 + w = 6$.

Remember
You can write some expressions in more than one way. All of these expressions mean to multiply 5 times a.

$5a$

$5 \times a$

$5(a)$

Example

> Patrick ran for 15 minutes and Shannon ran for m minutes. Together, they ran a total of 43 minutes. Write an equation that shows the total number of minutes Patrick and Shannon ran.
>
> _____

The total number of minutes they ran, 43, is the sum of the running times of each person, 15 (Patrick's time) and m (Shannon's time). So, $15 + m = 43$.

Answer: $15 + m = 43$

Patterns, Relationships, and Algebra

1

Cory wants to continue this number pattern.

2, 13, 24, 35, ___

What is the next number in the pattern?

A 11
B 43
C 46
D 59

2

Erica looks at a number pattern. She notices that each number is half the value of the number before it. If the first number in the pattern is 200, what is the fourth number in the pattern?

A 800
B 100
C 50
D 25

3

What is the *sixth* number in this pattern?

$\frac{1}{4}$, 1, 4, 16, ___, ?

A 24
B 64
C 128
D 256

4

Lance is reading a book. He read 7 pages the first day. Each day he reads twice as many pages as he did the day before. How many pages did Lance read on the fifth day?

A 112 pages
B 84 pages
C 56 pages
D 35 pages

Patterns, Relationships, and Algebra

5

Once a month Kayla mails the neighborhood newsletters. One month she mailed 50 newsletters. The next month she mailed n newsletters. Which expression shows the number of newsletters she mailed in all?

A $50 + n$

B $50 - n$

C $50 \times n$

D $50 \div n$

6

Amanda collected 6 times as many coins as Ray did. All together, they collected 42 coins. If c represents the number of coins Ray collected, which equation shows the total number of coins they collected together?

A $c + 6 = 42$

B $6c = 42$

C $6c + 6 = 42$

D $6c + c = 42$

7

Mr. Bennett ordered b bagels, a salad, and juice for lunch.

MENU

Bagel $0.95
Soup $2.75
Salad $5.95
Juice $1.25
Milk $1.00

Which expression shows how much Mr. Bennett spent for lunch?

A $0.95 + 5.95 + 1.25$

B $0.95b + 5.95 + 1.25$

C $b + 5.95 + 1.25$

D $0.95 + 5.95 + 1.25b$

8

Chelsea has $1.85 in change. She has q quarters, 2 dimes, and 3 nickels. Which equation describes Chelsea's change?

A $25q + 20 + 15 = 1.85$

B $0.25q + 0.20 + 0.15 = 1.85$

C $0.25 + 0.20 + 0.15 = q + 1.85$

D $0.25 + q + 0.20 + 0.15 = 1.85$

Skill Focus

Data, Statistics, and Probability

Interpret Graphs: Charts and Pictographs

Charts and *pictographs* display numeric data.

Charts A *table* displays data in columns and rows. The table below shows the number of movie DVDs a store has for four types of movies.

Type of Movie	Action	Comedy	Drama	Mystery
Number of DVDs	385	502	236	420

The top row lists the types of DVDs. The bottom row lists the number of DVDs. This display makes data easier to compare.

Pictographs Comparisons can also be done using a pictograph. A *pictograph* uses pictures or symbols. Each symbol has a value. A key below the pictograph tells the value of each symbol.

Hours Worked on Science Project

Team	Hours
A	🕐🕐🕐🕐
B	🕐🕐🕐
C	🕐🕐🕐🕐
D	🕐🕐

1 🕐 = 4 hours

Each clock represents 4 hours worked.

A half icon represents $\frac{1}{2}$ of 4, or 2 hours.

Team B worked ($2 \times 4 = 8$ hours) + ($\frac{1}{2}$ of 4 hours = 2 hours) = $8 + 2 = 10$ hours.

Remember
The word *of* means to multiply.
$\frac{1}{2}$ of $24 = \frac{1}{2} \times 24$
$= 12$

Example

Use the pictograph above to answer the question.

> How much longer did Team A work than Team C?
> _____

Team A worked $4 \times 4 = 16$ hours. Team C worked
($3 \times 4 = 12$ hours) + ($\frac{1}{2} \times 4 = 2$ hours) = $12 + 2 = 14$ hours.
$16 - 14 = 2$. Team A worked 2 hours longer than Team C.

Answer: 2 hours

Data, Statistics, and Probability

Interpret Graphs: Bar Graphs and Circle Graphs

Bar Graphs A *bar graph* uses vertical or horizontal bars to compare data. The vertical bar graph shows the salaries of 4 people in one town. Compare the top of each bar with the value shown on the left. The top of the bar for Person B is almost as high as $30,000 on the scale. This person's yearly salary is almost $30,000.

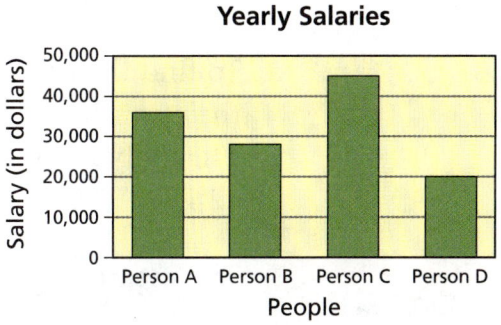

> **Remember**
> A *horizontal bar graph* has bars that go across a page, from left to right. To read it, compare the right end of each bar with the values on the horizontal axis.

Circle Graphs A *circle graph* shows how a piece of data relates to a whole set of data. Each section represents a part of the whole set of data.

Deanna asked four people what their favorite color is. She displays their answers on a circle graph. Deanna has 4 pieces of data. She finds what part of the whole each piece of data represents.

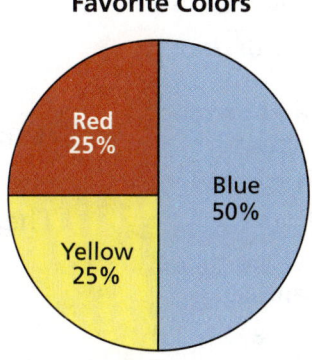

$\frac{1}{4} + \frac{1}{4} = \frac{2}{4}$ (blue) = 50%; $\frac{1}{4}$ (yellow) = 25%; $\frac{1}{4}$ (red) = 25%

Example

> Use the bar graph above to find the difference in the highest and lowest salary shown.
> _____

The highest salary shown is for Person C. The top of this bar is halfway between $40,000 and $50,000, so the salary is $45,000. The lowest salary shown is for Person D. The top of this bar is even with $20,000. 45,000 − 20,000 = 25,000, so the difference is $25,000.

Answer: $25,000

Data, Statistics, and Probability

Data, Statistics, and Probability

Mean, Median, Mode, and Range

Mean, median, mode, and range are ways to measure data.

To find the *mean*, or average, of a set of values (numbers), first find their sum. Then divide the sum by the number of values in the set. The daily high temperatures for six days in Center City were 70°F, 72°F, 70°F, 82°F, 78°F, and 84°F.

The mean is: $\frac{70 + 72 + 70 + 82 + 78 + 84}{6} = \frac{456}{6} = 76°F$

The *median* is the middle number when the data are arranged in order. If there are two middle numbers, the median is the average of the two middle numbers. The temperatures in order are 70°F, 70°F, 72°F, 78°F, 82°F, and 84°F. There are two numbers in the middle: 72°F and 78°F. The median is their average: $\frac{72°F + 78°F}{2} = 75°F$

The *mode* is the number that occurs most often. To find the mode, count how many times each number appears in the set. In the list of temperatures, 70°F appears twice. All other temperatures appear once. Therefore, 70°F is the mode.

The *range* of a set of data is the distance between the largest and smallest numbers. The lowest temperature is 70°F and the highest temperature is 84°F. The range is 84°F − 70°F or 14°F.

Remember
A *set of data* is all of the pieces of information you are given. Often a set of data is displayed in braces.
A set of data may have more than one mode. Example: {29, 14, 14, 29, 30}
A set of data may have no mode. Example: {16, 38, 21, 29}

Example

Find the median and the range for this set of data.
{15, 4, 4, 9, 5, 4, 12, 8, 7, 6}
Median: _____   Range: _____

The median is the middle number. Write the numbers in order: 4, 4, 4, 5, 6, 7, 8, 9, 12, 15. Find the number in the middle. There are two middle numbers, 6 and 7. The average of 6 and 7 is the median: $6 + 7 = \frac{13}{2} = 6.5$. The median is 6.5. The largest number is 15 and the smallest number is 4. The range is the difference between these two numbers. 15 − 4 = 11. The range is 11.

Answers: 6.5, 11

SKILL FOCUS

Data, Statistics, and Probability

Combinations

A *combination* is an arrangement of items in which order does not matter. For example, Wendy has some shirts and shorts. She chooses a red shirt and blue shorts to wear. This combination is the same as blue shorts and a red shirt.

Suppose Wendy is choosing her outfit from these items: a blue, red, or black top with jeans, shorts, or a skirt. How many combinations are possible? One way to solve this problem is with a *tree diagram*.

There are 9 possible combinations.

HINT
The counting principle uses multiplication. Be sure to multiply the number of choices. Do not add them.

You can also use the *counting principle* to find the number of possible combinations. There are 3 different tops (blue, red, black) and 3 different bottoms (jeans, shorts, skirt). The number of possible combinations is $3 \times 3 = 9$. What would happen if you add another choice, such as sandals or boots? Then the number of combinations would be $3 \times 3 \times 2 = 18$.

Example

> Robert is buying a new car. His color choices are: red, black, white, blue, or silver. He also has a choice between leather or cloth seats, and plain or fancy trim. How many different combinations of color, seats, and trim does Robert have to choose from?
> _____

You can answer this question quickly using the counting principle. Find the number of possibilities for each choice, then multiply them. There are 5 color choices, 2 seat choices, and 2 trim choices, so the total number of combinations is $5 \times 2 \times 2 = 20$.

Answer: 20

Data, Statistics, and Probability

Identify Possible Outcomes

An *outcome* is a result. For example, if you toss a coin, there are two *possible outcomes*, heads or tails. The coin will land on either heads or tails, so it is *certain* the outcome will be heads or tails.

A 1-to-6 number cube has 6 possible outcomes: 1, 2, 3, 4, 5, or 6. Each number occurs only one time, so you are equally likely to roll any of the numbers. It is not possible to roll a 7 since 7 is not on the number cube.

> **Remember**
> A list of all the possible outcomes is called a *sample space*. The sample space for this number cube is: 1, 2, 3, 4, 5, 6.

This spinner has 3 possible outcomes: red, yellow, or blue. The spinner is not equally likely to land on each color. Most of the spinner is red. The spinner is *most likely* to land on red. It is *least likely* to land on blue because the smallest section is blue.

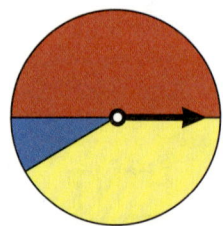

Example

Use the marbles in the bag to answer the questions. There are 5 blue, 4 red, 1 orange, and 2 white marbles.

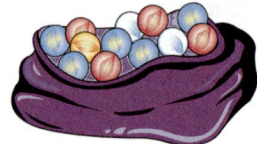

> You pick one marble from the bag without looking. What color are you most likely to pick?
> _____
>
> What color are you least likely to pick?
> _____
>
> Are you equally likely to pick any colors?
> _____
>
> What color is not possible to pick?
> _____

There are more blue marbles; you are most likely to pick blue. There is only 1 orange marble; you are least likely to pick orange. There is not an equal number of any color; you are not equally likely to pick any colors. Colors other than blue, red, white, and orange are not possible to pick.

Answers: blue; orange; no; answer can be any color that is not blue, red, white, or orange

Data, Statistics, and Probability

Probability

Probability is the likelihood that an outcome will occur. When an event is certain to happen, its probability is 1. A flipped coin will certainly land on *either* heads *or* tails, so its probability is 1. An impossible event has a probability of 0. The probability of a 1-to-6 number cube landing on 7 is impossible, so its probability is 0.

The probability that an event will occur is the ratio of the total number of *desired* outcomes to the total number of *possible* outcomes. Written as a fraction, the probability that an event will occur is expressed as $\frac{\text{total number of desired outcomes}}{\text{total number of possible outcomes}}$.

A bag has 10 marbles in it: 5 blue, 2 red, and 3 yellow. Pick a marble without looking. What is the probability you will choose a yellow marble?

The desired outcome is yellow, so there are 3 desired outcomes. There are 10 possible outcomes. The probability of choosing a yellow marble is $\frac{3}{10}$.

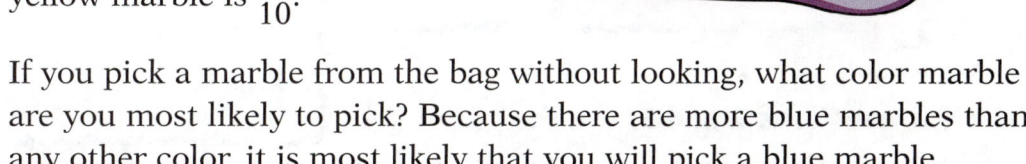

If you pick a marble from the bag without looking, what color marble are you most likely to pick? Because there are more blue marbles than any other color, it is most likely that you will pick a blue marble.

> **Remember**
> Probability can be expressed as a ratio, decimal, or percent. The probability of an outcome occurring is never less than 0% or more than 100%, so a probability expressed as a decimal will always be between 0 and 1.

Example

On any spin, what is the probability that the spinner will land on a B?

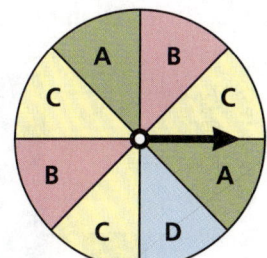

The number of desired outcomes is equal to the number of sections labeled "B." The number of possible outcomes is equal to the total number of sections. There are 2 sections marked "B" and 8 sections total. The probability is $\frac{2}{8}$ or $\frac{1}{4}$.

Answer: $\frac{1}{4}$

Data, Statistics, and Probability

1

The chart gives information about four volcanoes.

Height and Last Eruption of Volcanoes

Volcano	Country	Height (feet)	Last Eruption
Azuma	Japan	6700	1977
Mt. St. Helens	United States	8363	1991
El Misti	Peru	19,101	1870
Stromboli	Italy	3038	2003

When was the last eruption of Mt. St. Helens?

- **A** 8363
- **B** 1870
- **C** 3038
- **D** 1991

2

Which two planets are closest in size?

- **A** Earth and Mercury
- **B** Venus and Earth
- **C** Mercury and Mars
- **D** Mars and Venus

3

Which is *closest* to the diameter of Venus?

- **A** 6500 miles
- **B** 7000 miles
- **C** 7500 miles
- **D** 8000 miles

2–3

▼ **For questions 2 and 3, use the graph below.**

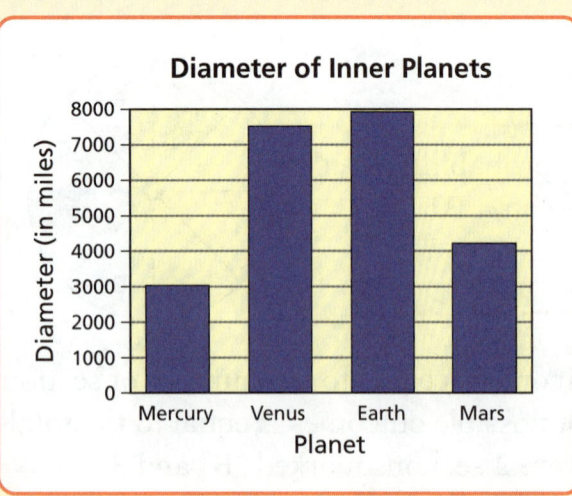

54   SKILL REVIEW

Data, Statistics, and Probability

4

The circle graph shows how Carrie spends the income from her after-school job.

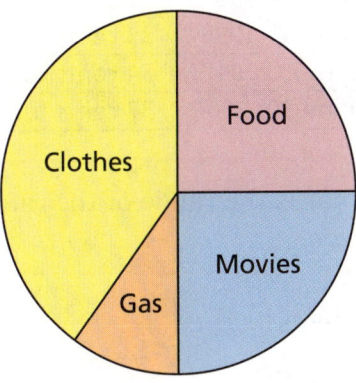

Carrie's Expenses

What does Carrie spend the largest portion of her income on?

A Food
B Movies
C Gas
D Clothes

5

Genny volunteers at a pet shelter. She recorded the number of pets adopted every day for two weeks and displayed the numbers in a stem-and-leaf plot.

Pets Adopted

1 | 1 2 2 4 7 8
2 | 0 0 1 3 4 5
3 | 0 1

Key: 1|1 means 11 pets

On how many days were more than 22 pets adopted?

A 2
B 3
C 5
D 7

6

Darla asked each of her classmates how tall he or she is. Which term describes the response that *most* students gave?

A mean
B median
C mode
D range

Data, Statistics, and Probability

7

The Acme Battery Company tested the battery lives of 7 different batteries. The number of hours each battery lasted is shown.

{13, 16, 11, 18, 15, 12, 16}

What is the median number of hours the batteries lasted?

A 7
B 14.4
C 15
D 16

8

The chart shows the most home runs hit in one season by baseball's greatest home-run hitters.

Most Home Runs in One Season

Number of Home Runs	Player	Year
73	Barry Bonds	2001
70	Mark McGwire	1998
66	Sammy Sosa	1998
65	Mark McGwire	1999
64	Sammy Sosa	2001

Which is closest to the mean number of home runs in the table?

A 9
B 11
C 66
D 68

9

The table gives the first-class U.S. Postal rates from 1991–2002.

U.S. Postal Rates

Feb. 3, 1991	29 cents for 1st oz.
Jan. 1, 1995	32 cents for 1st oz.
Jan. 10, 1999	33 cents for 1st oz.
Jan. 7, 2001	34 cents for 1st oz.
June 30, 2002	37 cents for 1st oz.

What is the range of the rates given?

A 8 cents
B 19 cents
C 29 cents
D 33 cents

10

A state uses two letters and one digit to create unique car license plates. A letter may be repeated, for example DD. The digits used are 0 through 9. How many unique car license plates can be made?

A $26 \times 26 \times 9$
B $26 + 26 + 10$
C $26 \times 25 \times 10$
D $26 \times 26 \times 10$

SKILL REVIEW

Data, Statistics, and Probability

11

Jamie is given one privilege for each chore he does. If he does the dishes, mows the lawn, or takes out the trash, he can watch television or play a video game. How many possible combinations of one chore and one privilege does Jamie have to choose from?

5	6	7	8
A	B	C	D

13

What is the probability of rolling an odd number on a 1-to-6 number cube?

$\frac{1}{6}$	$\frac{1}{3}$	$\frac{1}{2}$	1
A	B	C	D

12

What number is the spinner *least likely* to land on?

1	2	3	4
A	B	C	D

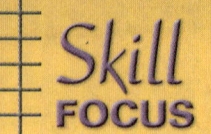

Skill Focus

Geometry and Measurement

The Coordinate Plane

The *coordinate plane* is a grid that shows positions on a plane. Positions on a coordinate plane are named by two coordinates, *x* and *y*. Because the coordinates are always listed (*x*, *y*) they are called an ordered pair.

To locate the point with coordinates (3, 1), start at the point with coordinates (0, 0). First move 3 spaces to the right along the *x*-axis. Then move 1 space up to 1 in the direction of the *y*-axis. The point with coordinates (3, 1) is Point *A*.

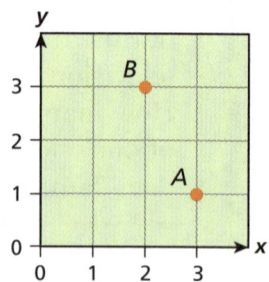

To find the ordered pair that identifies the location of point *B*, start at (0, 0). Point *B* is 2 spaces to the right of the origin and 3 spaces up. The ordered pair (2, 3) identifies the location of point *B*.

Remember
The point with coordinates (0, 0) is called the *origin*.

Example

What ordered pair identifies the location of the post office?

_____

Your location is (4, 1). Where are you?

_____

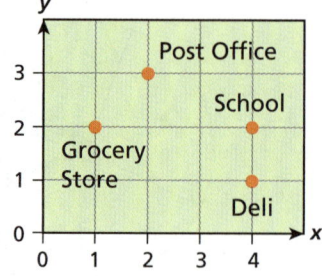

Start at (0, 0). Move 2 spaces to the right. The first number in the ordered pair is 2. Then move 3 spaces up. The second number in the ordered pair is 3. The post office is at position (2, 3).

Two places are at 4 along the *x*-axis. Only the deli is a 1 along the *y*-axis. So the deli is at (4, 1).

Answer: (2, 3), at the deli

Geometry and Measurement

Spatial Reasoning: Plane Figures

Sometimes you need to know what a plane, or two-dimensional, figure would look like from another view. You might also need to know what shapes would look like if pushed together. These types of questions deal with *spatial reasoning*.

Suppose you cut an isosceles trapezoid into 3 equilateral triangles.

If you separated the triangles and rearranged them, could you see how to put them back to form the trapezoid? There are several other shapes you can make with the triangles.

  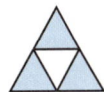

There are no rules about how to put shapes together to form a larger shape. But if you practice with cut-out shapes, you will begin to see some patterns.

Remember
Two sides of an *isosceles triangle* are the same length.
Three sides of an *equilateral triangle* are the same length.

Example

Show how you can make a square with these four triangles.

_____

Place the triangles so that four vertices meet at the center of the square.

Answer: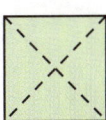

Geometry and Measurement

Spatial Reasoning: Solid Figures

Sometimes you are asked what a solid, or three-dimensional, figure would look like from another view. Or you may be given some plane figures and asked what solid figure you can form from them. Both of these situations deal with *spatial reasoning*.

Suppose you have these six plane figures.

What solid figure could you make using the plane figures? There are two squares and four rectangles. You could make a rectangular prism with the figures.

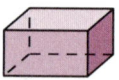

If you look at the rectangular prism from either end, you will see a square face. If you look at it from the top, bottom, left, or right, you will see a rectangular face.

> **Remember**
> A *face* of a solid figure is one of its flat surfaces. For example, a cube has 6 faces and each face is a square.

Example

> If you looked at this triangular prism from the back, what plane shape would you see: a square, a triangle, or a rectangle?
> _____

You can draw the prism and show the unseen faces using dotted lines. This shows you that the back face of the prism is a rectangle.

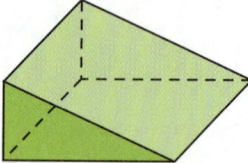

Answer: rectangle

Geometry and Measurement

Transformations

Remember
A slide is also called a *translation*.
A flip is also called a *reflection*.
A turn is also called a *rotation*.

You can move a figure to a new position using a slide or a flip, or by turning the figure. These movements are called *transformations*.

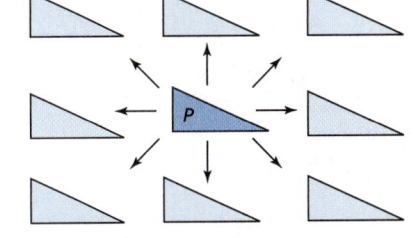

You can slide triangle *P* in any direction.

You can flip triangle *P* across a line of symmetry.

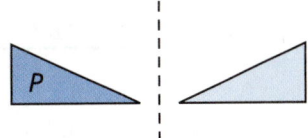

You can rotate triangle *P* clockwise or counterclockwise around a point.

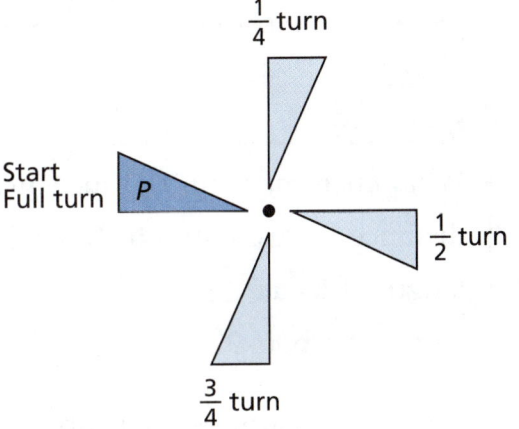

Example

What transformation describes the figure's change in position?
_____

A slide of the *R* would still look like an *R*. A flip would produce a mirror image of the *R*. A rotation turns the *R* around a point. So this figure has been rotated.

Answer: a rotation

Geometry and Measurement

Units of Measure: Length

Remember

Some *customary* units of length are:

inch, foot, yard, and mile.

Some *metric* units of length are:

millimeter, centimeter, meter, kilometer

Length is measured in *customary* and *metric* units. Long distances are measured in miles or kilometers. Short lengths are measured in inches, millimeters, and centimeters.

One inch is about $2\frac{1}{2}$ centimeters.

───── 1 inch
── 1 centimeter

One yard (36 inches) is just a little shorter than 1 meter. Lengths longer than this page are usually measured in feet, yards, or meters.

1 yard
1 meter
1 m = 39.3701 in.

One mile is a little over $1\frac{1}{2}$ kilometers. Long distances, such as the distance between two cities, are measured in miles or kilometers.

Example

> What customary unit of measure would be best for the
>
> distance from Boston to Dallas? _____
>
> length of a car? _____
>
> width of a book? _____
>
> What metric unit of measure would be best for the
>
> length of your little finger? _____
>
> distance from Chicago to San Diego? _____
>
> length of a bedroom? _____

Customary units: Boston to Dallas is a long distance; use miles. The length of a car is more than 12 inches; use feet. A book is less than a foot wide; use inches. Metric: Your little finger is less than a meter in length; use centimeters. Chicago to San Diego is a long distance; use kilometers. The length of a bedroom is far longer than your little finger; use meters.

Answer: miles, feet, inches, centimeters, kilometers, meters.

SKILL FOCUS

Geometry and Measurement

Perimeter

The *perimeter* of a shape is the distance around its outside edge. To find the perimeter of a shape, add the lengths of all its sides.

Remember
The perimeter of a rectangle is 2 × length + 2 × width.
The perimeter of a square is 4 × length of any side.

Look at the perimeter of these shapes.

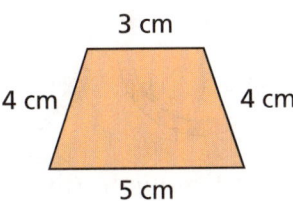

4 + 3 + 4 + 5 = 16
The perimeter of the shape is 16 centimeters.

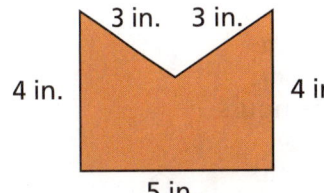

3 + 3 + 4 + 5 + 4 = 19
The perimeter of the shape is 19 inches.

Sometimes you know a shape's perimeter and need to find the length of a side.

If the perimeter of the triangle is 12 units, what is the length of the side labeled x?

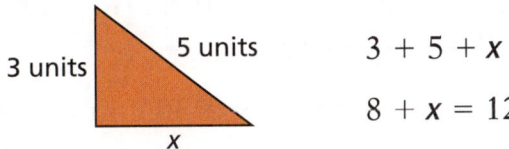

$3 + 5 + x = 12$

$8 + x = 12$

Since 3 + 5 = 8, the length of the side labeled x must be 4 units.

Example

Leslie plans to make this star-shaped polygon on the floor using colored tape. Each side of the star is the same length. Leslie has a 30-foot roll of tape. Is this enough tape to make the figure? _____

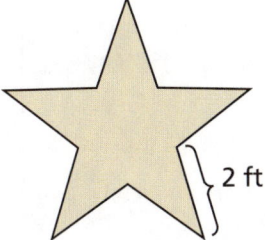

The 5-pointed star has 10 sides and each side measures 2 feet. The perimeter of the star is 2 feet × 10, or 20 feet. Since 20 < 30, she has enough tape.

Answer: Yes.

Geometry and Measurement

Time

The amount of time between two given times is called *elapsed time*.

What is the elapsed time between 11:30 A.M. and 1:15 P.M.?

One way to find the elapsed time is to divide the time into smaller units.

Time	Elapsed Time
11:30 - 12:30	1 hour
12:30 - 1:00	30 minutes
1:00 - 1:15	15 minutes

The total elapsed time equals
1 hour + 30 minutes + 15 minutes = 1 hour 45 minutes.

John worked on his homework for 45 minutes and then took a break. He worked again for 30 minutes. How long did John work on his homework all together?

45 minutes + 30 minutes = 75 minutes

To change 75 minutes into hours and minutes, divide by 60 minutes per hour. 75 ÷ 60 = 1 R15. The quotient is the number of hours and the remainder is the number of minutes. John worked for 1 hour 15 minutes.

> **Remember**
> The hours between 12:00 midnight and 12:00 noon are A.M. The hours between 12:00 noon and 12:00 midnight are P.M.

Example

> Jan goes to school from 9:30 A.M. to 3:40 P.M. How long is Jan at school? _____

From 9:30 A.M. to 3:30 P.M. is 6 hours. From 3:30 P.M. to 3:40 P.M. is 10 minutes. Jan is at school for 6 hours and 10 minutes.

Answer: 6 hours 10 minutes

Geometry and Measurement

Scale Drawings

When you use a map to find the distance from one city to another, you are using a *scale drawing*. The *scale* of the drawing relates the measurements of the drawing to the actual measurements of the object.

> **HINT**
> The ruler distance between two places on a map, the straight distance, is often called "as the crow flies," because the crow flies in a straight line. Roads are often not straight. So the driving distance is a little longer than the straight-line distance.

Use your inch ruler to measure the distance from City A to City B. The straight-line distance between the cities on the map is exactly one inch. The map scale says that 1 inch equals 50 miles, so the two cities are about 50 miles apart.

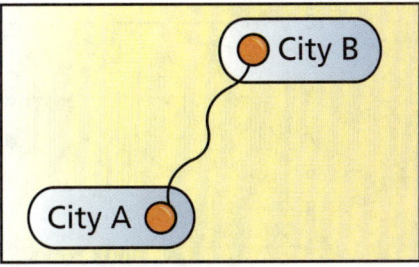

1 inch = 50 miles

When the measurements of a model of an object relate directly to those of a real object, the model is called a *scale model*. This scale model of a car is on display in a shop.

If the model van is 9 inches long, how long is the actual van? The scale says that every inch on the model equals 2 feet on the actual van. So the actual car length is 9 × 2 feet, or 18 feet long.

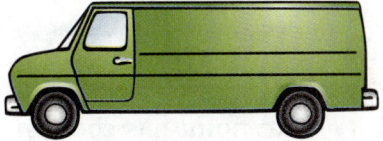

1 inch = 2 feet

Example

> A scale model of a storage shed is 5 inches by 6 inches. The scale factor is 1 inch = 3 feet. What is the length and width of the actual shed? _____

On the model, one side of the shed is 5 inches. 5 × 3 feet = 15 feet. The other side of the model is 6 inches. 6 × 3 = 18 feet. The actual storage shed is 15 feet by 18 feet.

Answer: 15 feet by 18 feet

Geometry and Measurement

1–2

Use the coordinate grid below for questions 1 and 2.

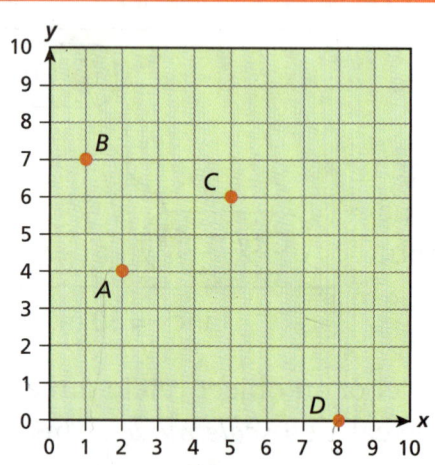

1

What point has coordinates (1, 7)?

- **A** A
- **B** B
- **C** C
- **D** D

2

What are the coordinates of Point *D*?

- **A** (0, 8)
- **B** (1, 8)
- **C** (8, 0)
- **D** (8, 1)

3

Which shapes could be used to make a pentagon like the one above?

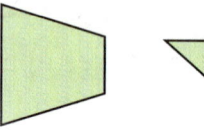

A

B

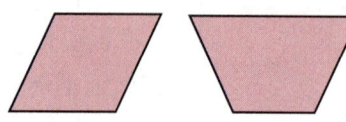

C

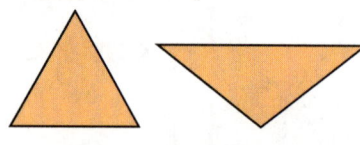

D

66   SKILL REVIEW

Geometry and Measurement

4 Suppose you have this figure.

Which shapes could be its faces?

- A (2 triangles, 2 squares)
- B (1 triangle, 3 rectangles)
- C (2 triangles, 3 rectangles)
- D (2 triangles, 3 rectangles)

5 Which unit of measurement is *best* for measuring the length of a school gym?

- A feet
- B inches
- C kilometers
- D millimeters

6

The shape on the left was moved to make the shape on the right.

What kind of transformation was used?

- A Slide
- B Flip
- C Turn
- D Resize

7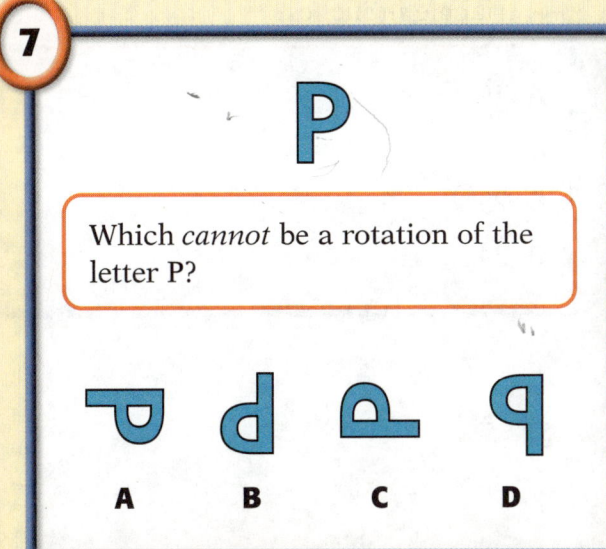

Which *cannot* be a rotation of the letter P?

A B C D

Geometry and Measurement

8

Which unit of measurement is *best* for measuring the distance between two cities?

A yards
B miles
C meters
D centimeters

9

What is the perimeter of the triangle in inches?

(Triangle with sides 5 in., 8 in., 10 in.)

A 19
B 21
C 23
D 24

10

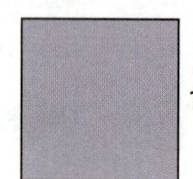
Perimeter = 16 m

The perimeter of the square is 16 meters. What is the length of one side?

A 2 m
B 4 m
C 8 m
D 10 m

11

Adolfo watched a movie that was 107 minutes long. How long was the movie in hours and minutes?

A 1 hour, 7 minutes
B 1 hour, 47 minutes
C 2 hours, 7 minutes
D 2 hours, 17 minutes

68   SKILL REVIEW

Geometry and Measurement

12

Brandy's soccer game started at 3:30 P.M. and ended at 5:10 P.M. How long did the game last?

A 1 hour, 40 minutes

B 1 hour 50 minutes

C 2 hours 10 minutes

D 2 hours 20 minutes

13

Priscilla is looking at this map of Tennessee.

Memphis

Scale: 1 inch = 40 mi

According to the map, what is the actual distance from Nashville to Memphis?

A 8 miles

B 45 miles

C 160 miles

D 200 miles

14

Jerry built a model of a 36-foot-long boat. He used the scale: 1 inch = 3 feet.

36 feet

What is the length of Jerry's scale model?

A 12 inches

B 24 inches

C 86 inches

D 108 inches

Mathematics Problem Solving

DIRECTIONS

Read each question carefully. Then answer the question or work the problem. Mark the space for your answer.

SAMPLE A

What is the value of the 6 in 26,853?

A 6
B 60
C 600
D 6000

SAMPLE B

Yellow   Yellow

Red   Green

What fraction of the marbles are yellow?

$\frac{1}{4}$ $\frac{1}{2}$ $\frac{1}{3}$ $\frac{3}{4}$
A   B   C   D

---

1 Donna's car has one hundred four thousand, five hundred miles on it. Which number is equivalent to one hundred four thousand, five hundred?

A 104,050
B 104,500
C 140,500
D 145,000

2 Which number is one-tenth *greater* than 20.35?

A 20.36
B 20.45
C 21.35
D 30.35

Mathematics Problem Solving

3

In the figure below, each triangle is the same size.

What fractional part of the whole figure is shaded?

$\frac{1}{4}$ $\frac{1}{3}$ $\frac{1}{2}$ $\frac{2}{3}$
A   B   C   D

4

Tanya stated that the winner of the school election received less than 500 votes. Which number is *closest* to her statement?

A 455 votes
B 481 votes
C 500 votes
D 506 votes

5

Which number is equivalent to $\frac{12}{30}$?

0.4   0.5 $\frac{1}{4}$ $\frac{1}{5}$
A   B   C   D

6

The scale below is balanced.

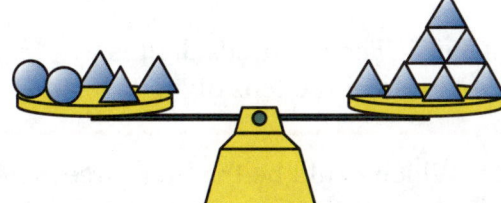

How many pyramids should be placed on the right side of the scale below to balance the scale?

A 1 pyramid
B 2 pyramids
C 3 pyramids
D 4 pyramids

Mathematics Problem Solving

7

When Rachel's family moved, they received a new phone number. She told her friends that the last four digits stayed the same, but the first three digits changed. Rachel gave her friends the following clues so they could guess the first three digits of her new phone number:

Clue 1: All 3 digits are odd.

Clue 2: The difference between the hundreds digit and the ones digit is four.

Clue 3: The hundreds digit is a multiple of the tens digit.

Which could be the first three digits of Rachel's new phone number?

A 537

B 733

C 824

D 935

8

Harold solved the subtraction problem below.

$$4155 - 327$$

Harold got an answer of 4123. He knew that this answer was wrong. What was one way Harold might have known that he got the wrong answer?

A The number should have 5 digits in it.

B The number should be less than 4000.

C The number should be greater than 5000.

D The number should have a 2 in the ones place.

9

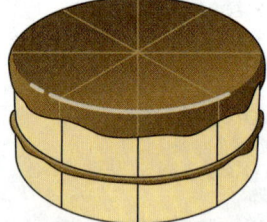

If no more cuts are made, how many people can share this cake equally?

A 3 or 5 people   **C** 4 or 7 people

B 2 or 4 people   **D** 5 or 6 people

Mathematics Problem Solving

10

The chart gives the prices of the items that are used to make a bracelet.

Craft World: Price List

Item	Cost (including tax)
String	$0.25 per inch
Clasps	$1.00 each
Beads	$0.60 each
Jewels	$0.90 each

Sandy fills out the order form below. How much will the items needed to make the bracelet cost altogether?

Craft World: Order Form

Item	Quantity
String	8 inches
Clasps	1
Beads	6
Jewels	3

A $9.30

B $8.30

C $7.60

D $6.70

11

Which list shows the values in order from *least* to *greatest*?

A $\frac{1}{4}$, 0.6, $\frac{2}{5}$, 0.3

B $\frac{1}{4}$, $\frac{2}{5}$, 0.3, 0.6

C 0.3, 0.6, $\frac{1}{4}$, $\frac{2}{5}$

D $\frac{1}{4}$, 0.3, $\frac{2}{5}$, 0.6

12

Which expression should go in the box to make the number sentence true?

$$9 + 342 = \square$$

A 342 ÷ 9

B 342 − 9

C 342 × 9

D 342 + 9

Posttest

Mathematics Problem Solving

13

Kim answered 46 out of 50 questions correctly on her test. She received 2 points for every correct answer and she lost 1 point for every incorrect answer. What was Kim's test score?

A 86
C 88
B 92
D 96

14

Which number is *greater* than $2\frac{1}{5}$ and *less* than $2\frac{1}{4}$?

A 2.10
C 2.30
B 2.23
D 2.32

15

Mandy missed the bus to school so she had to walk. It takes her 20 minutes to get to school on the bus. It takes Mandy 1 hour to walk to school. How many times longer does it take for Mandy to walk to school than to take the bus?

A two times longer
B three times longer
C four times longer
D six times longer

16

Aaron wants to go to the observation deck at the top of the tallest building in the city. An elevator takes him to the top floor and he climbs the stairs to the deck.

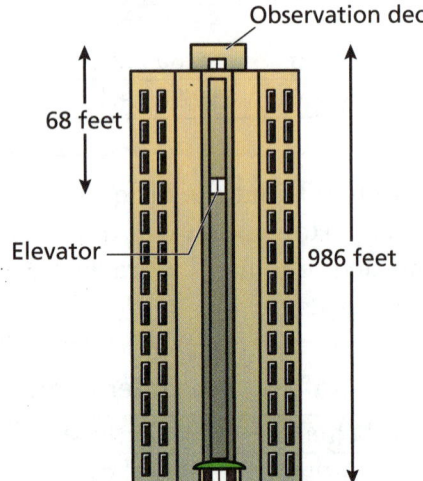

Which equation could be used to find the distance, d, Aaron traveled on the elevator?

A $986 - 68 = d$
B $986 + 68 = d$
C $d + 986 = 68$
D $d - 68 = 986$

Mathematics Problem Solving

17

Cindy is collecting leaves for a science project. She has collected 135 leaves. She needs a total of 300 leaves to finish the project. What fraction of the total number of leaves has Cindy collected?

$\frac{3}{10}$ $\frac{9}{20}$ $\frac{11}{20}$ $\frac{4}{5}$
A   B   C   D

18

The choir is raising money for a field trip. They shade a circle to show the fraction of their goal that they have reached. Which figure *best* represents 35% of their goal?

A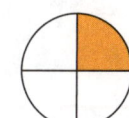

C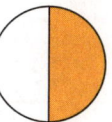

B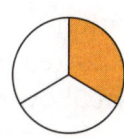

D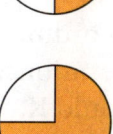

19

Eric buys 300 cookies and shares them equally among the 12 teams in his volleyball league. Which expression could *not* be used to determine how many cookies each team received?

A $\frac{300}{12}$

B $300 \div 12$

C $300 - 12$

D $12\overline{)300}$

20

What is the value of the 3 in 98.203?

A 3 hundreds

B 3 thousands

C 3 hundredths

D 3 thousandths

Mathematics Problem Solving

21

Dan has five coins in his pocket. They have a total value of 42¢.

How many dimes does Dan have?

A 1   C 3
B 2   D 4

23

In the figure below, each triangle is the same size.

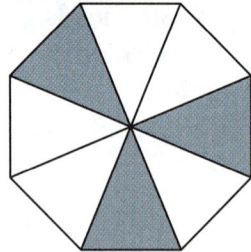

What fractional part of the whole figure is shaded?

$\frac{1}{3}$ $\frac{3}{8}$ $\frac{1}{2}$ $\frac{3}{5}$
A   B   C   D

22

The chart below gives the shipping cost of a package based on its weight.

Shipping Costs

Weight (pounds)	Cost ($)
Less than 3 lbs	$4.25
Between 3 and 5 lbs	$6.60
Between 5 and 9 lbs	$8.49

Which is the *least* expensive to ship?

A Five 2-lb boxes

B Three 4-lb boxes

C One 1-lb box and two 6-lb boxes

D One 4-lb box and three 2-lb boxes

24

$(3 + 5) \times 4 - 1$

According to the rules for order of operations, which operation should Kayla do first to correctly work the problem shown above?

A $3 + 5$ C $4 - 1$
B 8×4 D 5×4

Mathematics Problem Solving

25

Mr. Moore's students used a number rule to construct the number table below. Each pair of numbers in the table satisfies the rule.

A	B
3	1
7	5
4	2
2	0

What is the rule to get from a number in the "A" column to a number in the "B" column?

A A ÷ 2 **C** A − 2
B A + 2 **D** A · 2

27

Shondra goes to a laundry to wash her clothes. She buys tokens to use in the washing machines. ● is a token for a 75¢ wash and ● is a token for a $1.25 wash.

Shondra buys 6 blue tokens and 3 red tokens. How much does Shondra spend altogether for tokens?

A $3.75 **C** $6.25
B $4.50 **D** $8.25

26

The chart shows the number of edges a prism has.

Prisms

Name of 3-Dimensional Solid	Number of Edges
Triangular prism	9
Rectangular prism	12
Pentagonal prism	15
Hexagonal prism	?

How many edges does a hexagonal prism have?

A 17 **C** 19
B 18 **D** 21

28

Keith asks 15 students what they ate for lunch. Two out of every five students say they ate pasta. How many students ate pasta?

A 5 students
B 6 students
C 9 students
D 12 students

Posttest

Mathematics Problem Solving

29

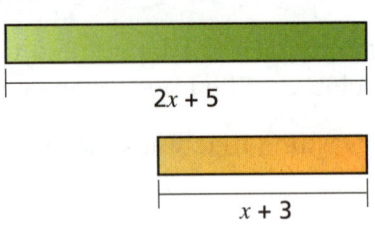

2x + 5

x + 3

Which expression can be used to find how much longer the green stick is than the orange stick?

A $x + 2$
B $x - 2$
C $2x + 5 - x + 3$
D $(2x + 5) + (x + 3)$

30

Dave holds a basketball 6 feet above the ground and drops it. Each time the ball bounces it reaches a height that is half the last bounce. The chart gives the height of the first three bounces.

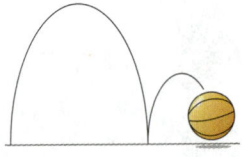

Basketball Experiment

Bounce	Height
first	3 ft
second	$1\frac{1}{2}$ ft
third	$\frac{3}{4}$ ft

If the pattern continues, about how high will the ball rise on the fifth bounce?

$\frac{1}{16}$ ft $\frac{1}{8}$ ft $\frac{3}{16}$ ft $\frac{3}{8}$ ft
A   B   C   D

31

Iris is the goalie for her school's soccer team. The graph shows the number of goals attempted and the number of goals that Iris allowed during the games she played this season.

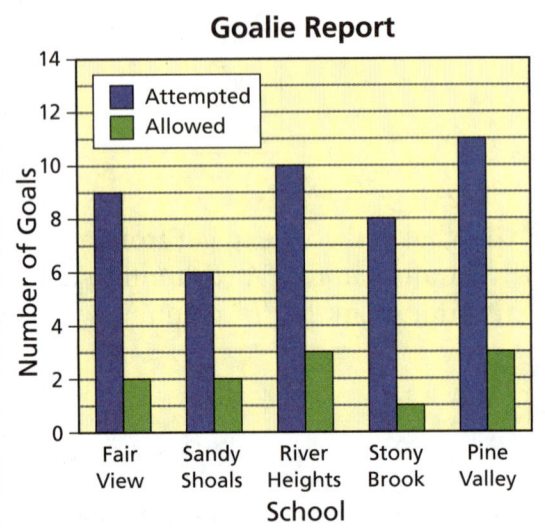

Goalie Report

How many goals did Iris allow this season?

A 11
B 22
C 33
D 44

78   MATHEMATICS PROBLEM SOLVING

Mathematics Problem Solving

32

Marvin rides his bike to the bus stop. He then takes a bus to school. Marvin can choose one of three routes to get to the bus stop and one of four buses to get to school.

How many different combinations of one bike route and one bus can Marvin choose from?

4	7	10	12
A	B	C	D

33

Will surveys 28 classmates about what kind of pets they like best. He records the results in the graph below.

Favorite Pets

- Birds (9)
- Cats (7)
- Fish (2)
- Dogs (10)

What kind of pet do 25% of the students in Will's class like best?

A Dogs   C Fish
B Cats   D Birds

34

The chart shows how much money Roy earned from babysitting.

Money Earned Babysitting

Month	Total
January	$12.00
February	$28.00
March	$14.50
April	$22.00
May	$17.50
June	$32.00

What was the mean (average) amount of money Roy earned each month from January to June?

A $19.75

B $20.00

C $21.00

D $22.50

Mathematics Problem Solving

35

The pictograph shows the total number of books read by the students at Harbor Middle School.

Harbor Middle School Read-a-thon

Grade	Number of Books Read
5	📚
6	📚
7	📚📚
8	📚

Each 📕 represents 100 books.

How many books did the students at Harbor Middle School read during the Read-a-thon?

- **A** 30 books
- **B** 290 books
- **C** 2500 books
- **D** 2900 books

36

The sides of a cube are painted. Two sides are painted blue and four sides are painted red.

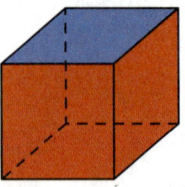

In 100 fair rolls, what number of times would the cube be expected to land with a blue side face up?

- **A** Between 10 and 20 times
- **B** Between 20 and 40 times
- **C** Between 40 and 60 times
- **D** Between 60 and 80 times

37

This chart shows the cost of one airline ticket at different times of the year and for different classes.

Air Fares

Class	Winter	Summer
First Class	$440	$525
Business Class	$325	$415
Coach	$265	$325

Bill and Tina are traveling business class this summer. How much will it cost for *both* of them to fly?

- **A** $415
- **B** $650
- **C** $830
- **D** $1050

Mathematics Problem Solving

38

Nick has an 8-inch, a 10-inch, and a 12-inch frying pan in his kitchen. He keeps the covers in a drawer. If Nick removes a cover from the drawer without looking, what is the probability that the cover will fit the 10-inch frying pan?

$\frac{1}{9}$ $\frac{1}{6}$ $\frac{1}{3}$ $\frac{2}{3}$
A   B   C   D

40

What is the perimeter of the figure?

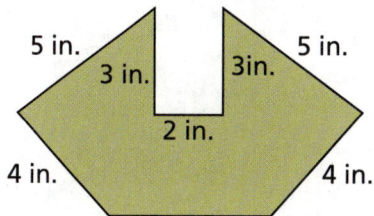

A 25 in.   C 31 in.
B 28 in.   D 33 in.

39

Which ordered pair names the location of point S?

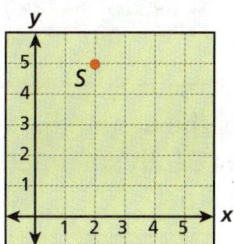

A (2, 2)
B (2, 5)
C (5, 2)
D (5, 5)

41

The figure below is a flat piece of paper.

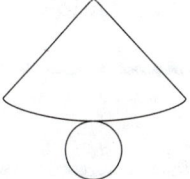

Which 3-dimensional figure can the paper be folded into?

A 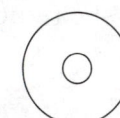   C

B    D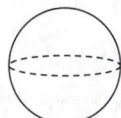

Posttest   81

Mathematics Problem Solving

42

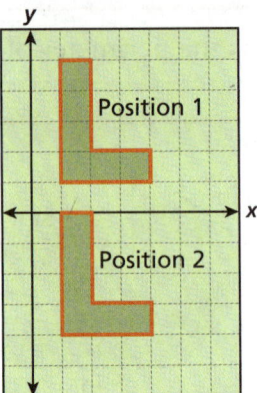

Which transformation can be used to move the figure on the grid from Position 1 to Position 2 in one step?

A Reflection (flip)

B Rotation (turn)

C Dilation (enlargement)

D Translation (slide)

43

Anna leaves school for a doctor's appointment at 10:35 A.M. and returns 2 hours and 40 minutes later. At what time does she return to school?

A 1:15 A.M.

B 2:15 A.M.

C 1:15 P.M.

D 2:15 P.M.

44

Use your inch ruler and this picture to help you answer this question.

Molly and Jim are riding kayaks down a river.

What is the actual distance between Molly's helmet and Jim's helmet?

A 10 yards

B 15 yards

C 20 yards

D 25 yards

Mathematics Problem Solving

45

Use your centimeter ruler and this picture to help you answer this question.

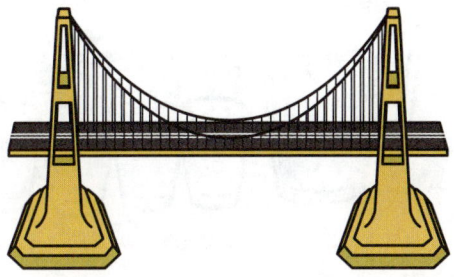

This is a scale drawing of a bridge that is 1200 meters long. What is the scale of the drawing?

A 1 cm
⊢—⊣
0   60 m
Scale

B 1 cm
⊢—⊣
0   70 m
Scale

C 1 cm
⊢—⊣
0   120 m
Scale

D 1 cm
⊢—⊣
0   200 m
Scale

46

What does this figure look like when viewed from the front?

A

B

C

D

Posttest

83

Mathematics Problem Solving

47

The area of the blue square is 16 square inches.

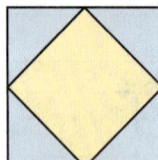

If the area of each blue triangle is 2 square inches, what is the area of the yellow diamond?

A 4 square inches

B 8 square inches

C 12 square inches

D 14 square inches

48

When this pitcher is full, it contains enough water to fill 8 pint-sized glasses.

The water in this pitcher is divided equally into 24 pint-sized glasses. What fraction of the total capacity of each glass is filled with water?

$\frac{1}{6}$ $\frac{1}{4}$ $\frac{1}{3}$ $\frac{1}{2}$
A   B   C   D

Mathematics Procedures

DIRECTIONS ▶

Read each question or problem carefully. Then answer the question or work the problem. Mark the space for your answer. If a correct answer is not here, mark the space for NH.

SAMPLE A

43.3
+ 6.6

A 34.3
B 48.9
C 49.0
D 49.9
E NH

SAMPLE B

A community swimming pool is divided into two sections, one for adults and one for children. The adults' pool holds 19,250 gallons of water. The children's pool holds 4650 gallons of water.

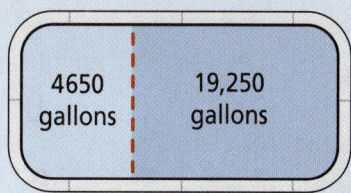

How much water do the two pools hold altogether?

A 14,600 gallons
B 22,800 gallons
C 23,900 gallons
D 24,900 gallons
E NH

1

324
42
+ 67

A 323
B 433
C 423
D 453
E NH

2

6.9 × 1.03 = ☐

A 0.7107
B 0.710
C 7.107
D 7.701
E NH

Posttest

85

Mathematics Procedures

3) $\frac{4}{7} - \frac{3}{7} = \square$

1	$\frac{7}{14}$	$\frac{43}{7}$	$\frac{1}{7}$	$\frac{3}{7}$
A	B	C	D	E

4) 27 × 43

453	821	961	1061	NH
A	B	C	D	E

5) 3195 − 628

2567	2577	2573	2823	NH
A	B	C	D	E

6) $\frac{5}{9} \times \frac{2}{3} = \square$

$\frac{7}{12}$	$\frac{7}{27}$	$\frac{10}{12}$	$\frac{10}{27}$	$\frac{15}{18}$
A	B	C	D	E

7) 41.97 + 6.34 = $\square$

47.31	48.31	35.63	48.63	NH
A	B	C	D	E

8) $7\frac{3}{8} + 4\frac{6}{8} = \square$

12	11	$12\frac{1}{8}$	$11\frac{1}{8}$	$12\frac{9}{8}$
A	B	C	D	E

9) $\frac{5}{6} - \frac{2}{3} = \square$

1	$\frac{7}{3}$	$\frac{7}{9}$	$\frac{1}{2}$	$\frac{1}{6}$
A	B	C	D	E

Mathematics Procedures

10

732 ÷ 9 = ☐

A 81 R3
B 80 R3
C 80 R2
D 81
E NH

11

34.76 − 2.89 = ☐

A 32.97
B 31.87
C 37.65
D 32.87
E NH

12

1.09 × 0.03 = ☐

A 0.127
B 0.327
C 0.0127
D 0.00327
E NH

13

531 ÷ 9 = ☐

A 53 R1
B 59
C 59 R1
D 60
E NH

14

$24 \times \frac{1}{4}$ = ☐

$24\frac{1}{4}$	$6\frac{1}{4}$	20	6	$4\frac{1}{6}$
A	B	C	D	E

15

45.6 ÷ 3 = ☐

A 13.5   D 15.2
B 12.1   E NH
C 15.3

Posttest

87

Mathematics Procedures

16

$\frac{2}{3} \times 6 = \square$

$\frac{12}{18}$	$\frac{2}{18}$	$\frac{8}{3}$	9	4
A	B	C	D	E

17

Harriet buys 15 cartons of eggs. Each carton contains one dozen eggs.

How many eggs does Harriet buy altogether?

A 220   D 160
B 180   E NH
C 170

18

A basketball weighs 21.16 ounces. A baseball weighs 5.12 ounces.

21.16 ounces   5.12 ounces

How much more in ounces does a basketball weigh than a baseball?

A 15.04   D 16.14
B 16.02   E NH
C 16.08

19

Joy ate $\frac{3}{8}$ of this pizza for lunch.

She ate an additional $\frac{4}{8}$ of the pizza for dinner.

What fraction of the total pizza did Joy eat?

$\frac{7}{8}$	$\frac{7}{16}$	$\frac{8}{12}$	$\frac{12}{64}$	$\frac{7}{64}$
A	B	C	D	E

Mathematics Procedures

20

A gallon of water weighs 8.3 pounds.

How many pounds of water does it take to fill an empty 25-gallon barrel?

A 108
B 118.8
C 206.5
D 207.5
E NH

22

A total of 315 students attend Washington Elementary School. Of those students, $\frac{1}{9}$ are in band class.

How many students at Washington Elementary are in band class?

A 25
B 35
C 40
D 49
E NH

21

Michael pays $4.68 for a carton of 12 bottles of water.

If there is no tax, how much does each bottle of water cost?

A 37¢
B 39¢
C 42¢
D 47¢
E NH

23

Nao wins a prize of $125.00. He decides to share the prize with his parents and his sister. Nao gives his sister $20.00 and keeps $40.00 for himself. He divides the rest equally and buys a gift for his mother and a gift for his father.

How much money did Nao spend on each gift?

A $42.50
B $25.00
C $65.00
D $32.50
E NH

Mathematics Procedures

24

In 1954, the height of Mt. Everest was measured at 29,028 feet. In 1999, the height of Mt. Everest was measured again with better instruments. The new height of Mt. Everest is 7 feet higher than the height measured in 1954.

What is the new height of Mt. Everest in feet?

A 29,098
B 29,035
C 29,028
D 29,021
E NH

25

Leroy goes to the market to buy fruit. When he weighs the fruit in the basket, the scale reads 4.27 pounds. The basket alone weighs 0.35 pound.

How many pounds does the fruit weigh without the basket?

A 3.27   D 4.62
B 3.92   E NH
C 3.97

26

Mario had $5.00 at the beginning of the week. He spent $\frac{1}{5}$ of his money on snacks and $\frac{2}{5}$ on school supplies. What fraction of the money does Mario have left?

$\frac{1}{5}$ $\frac{2}{5}$ $\frac{3}{5}$ $\frac{4}{5}$ $\frac{6}{5}$
A   B   C   D   E

Mathematics Procedures

27

Judy buys 420 postage stamps. The stamps come in sheets of 30 stamps each.

How many sheets of stamps does Judy buy?

A 13
B 14
C 26
D 71
E NH

28

Lori's parents drove their car 58,424 miles before they went on vacation. While on vacation, they drove another 1677 miles.

How many miles have Lori's parents driven their car altogether?

A 56,747
B 58,424
C 60,024
D 61,001
E NH

Mathematics Procedures

29

Dustin and his friend are snacking on a bag of sunflower seeds. Dustin eats $\frac{1}{2}$ of the seeds in the bag. His friend eats $\frac{1}{3}$ of the seeds in the bag.

Dustin: 1/2 of seeds
Dustin's friend: 1/3 of seeds

What fraction of the sunflower seeds do Dustin and his friend eat in all?

$\frac{5}{6}$	$\frac{2}{3}$	$\frac{1}{3}$	$\frac{1}{5}$	$\frac{1}{6}$
A	B	C	D	E

30

On Monday, *Timothy's Tires* sold 268 tires. Each customer bought four tires.

How many customers did Timothy have on Monday?

A 27
B 42
C 47
D 62
E NH

Mathematics Procedures

31

The Math Club is producing an instructional CD using music as a class project. So far, the club has produced 3 lessons.

CD Tracks	Time (minutes:seconds)
1. Rock 'n' Roll Algebra	12:15
2. Hip Hop Number Sense	14:38
3. Geometry Tango	11:19

How long in minutes and seconds is the CD?

A 37:02
B 38:12
C 37:12
D 38:02
E NH

32

Ryan lives 4.5 miles from school. He rides his bike to school every morning. On Tuesday morning, he had ridden his bike 3.24 miles when he got a flat tire.

How far was Ryan from school when he got the flat tire?

A 0.26 miles
B 0.36 miles
C 1.26 miles
D 1.36 miles
E NH

Test Best® for the Stanford 10 Reference Sheet
Intermediate 2

CUSTOMARY MEASURES: CONVERSION CHART

Length:
- 1 foot (ft) = 12 inches (in.)
- 1 yard (yd) = 3 feet
- 1 mile (mi) = 5280 feet

Weight:
- 1 pound (lb) = 16 ounces
- 1 ton (t) = 2000 pounds

Capacity:
- 1 cup (c) = 8 fluid ounces (fl oz)
- 1 pint (pt) = 2 cups
- 1 quart (qt) = 2 pints
- 1 gallon (gal) = 4 quarts

METRIC MEASURES

Length:
- 1 meter (m) = 100 centimeters (cm)
- 1 kilometer (km) = 1000 meters

Mass:
- 1 kilogram (kg) = 1000 grams (g)

Capacity:
- 1 liter (L) = 1000 milliliters (mL)

TEMPERATURE

Customary Measure
- Degrees Fahrenheit (°F)
  - Water freezes at 32 °F
  - Water boils at 212 °F

Metric Measure
- Degrees Celsius (°C)
  - Water freezes at 0 °C
  - Water boils at 100 °C

Test Best® *for the Stanford 10* Reference Sheet
Intermediate 2

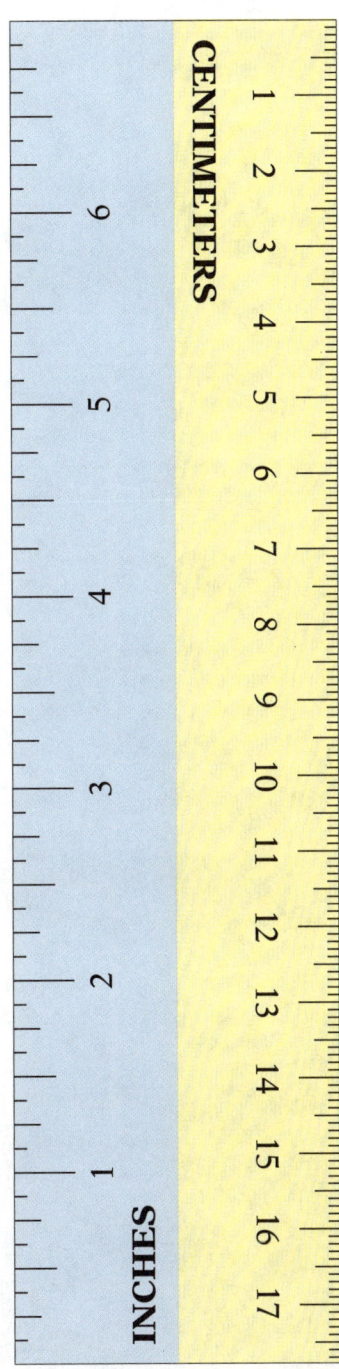